How to be
FRENCH

First published in hardback in 2015 by Old Street Publishing Ltd,
Yowlestone House, Tiverton EX16 8LN
www.oldstreetpublishing.co.uk

This paperback edition published 2015

ISBN 978 1 910400 19 7

10 9 8 7 6 5 4 3 2 1

A CIP catalogue record for this title is available from the British Library.

Printed and bound in Great Britain by CPI Group (UK) Ltd, Croydon, CR0 4YY

How to be FRENCH

ALEX QUICK

with Cyn Bataille

Contents

FRENCH BEHAVIOUR

FRENCH WELL-BEING

FRENCH ACTIVITIES

FRENCH PLACES

FRENCH CRIMES

FRENCH LANGUAGE

FRENCH SPORTS AND ENTERTAINMENT

Introduction

There has been a great deal of interest recently in the French way of life. Particularly in the way of life of French women and their children. You may have encountered the sort of titles: *French Women Don't Get Old and Ugly*, *French Children Don't Knife Their Playmates*, *How to Wear Your Little Black Dress Past the Age of 117*, *The French Women Don't Become Morbidly Obese Cookbook*.

However, while French women may be admirable in many respects, this book is unable to add to the roster of their achievements. Instead, it aims to describe the things that Frenchwomen – and Frenchmen – actually do. We think it's more interesting to show the real France, a complex place full of people who are all shapes and sizes, and who spend their time in sometimes rather surprising ways: practising French martial arts, brewing their own firewater, persecuting small birds, wrapping themselves in seaweed, kissing Fanny's bottom, urinating in public, killing each other over truffles, and mercilessly satirizing themselves.

Once you've attempted the 102 things detailed here, you may well be thinner, younger and more good-looking, with well-behaved children and a decluttered wardrobe. If that's the case, we are overjoyed for you. But we probably didn't have anything to do with it.

Alex Quick and Cyn Bataille, Norwich and Nimes

French Food and Drink

1.

Talk About Food

❊

Why not start where the French themselves would start? That is, with food?

There is a very telling moment in *Asterix and the Olympic Games* – written, of course, by that great French genius René Goscinny – when Asterix and Obelix are dining with the Gaulish Olympic team at a restaurant in Greece. As they tuck into their stuffed vine-leaves, Obelix says to Asterix: 'Do you remember the little restaurant in Lugdunum where we had that delicious veal?'

For the French, food is the greatest of all topics of conversation, and there is no better time to talk about food than when one is engaged in eating it. Regional specialities, the best way to prepare a certain dish, legendary meals of yore, impossible-to-obtain ingredients, the best markets, chefs, wines, vegetarianism and its perverseness: the range of topics is effectively unbounded. It's surprising the

French talk about anything else, and sometimes they don't.

A famous experiment was carried out in which a group of Americans and a group of French were shown a picture of a chocolate cake and asked what emotion it elicited. The Americans, predominantly, said 'guilt', and the French, predominantly, said 'celebration'. That really says it all. American puritanism seeks to mortify and tame the body; French sensuality seeks to indulge and celebrate it. And the French still wind up thinner than the Americans. How do they pull that off?

Perhaps it's because the French sit down to eat, enjoy it, take it seriously and regard it as a way to spend time with friends and family. They savour it, they know about it, they appreciate it. They don't snack all day, alone, on foods that have little intrinsic interest or personality.

Not to have an opinion about food, or to regard it as mere fuel, is the purest form of French nihilism.

2.

Eat Things That Look Like Things

❁

In Anglophone lands, we prefer to eat things that look nothing like things. In France, they are not so squeamish. Witness *tête de veau*. This is a real calf's head, reclining in a dish and looking dejected. Jacques Chirac is said to munch with pleasure on *tête de veau*, possibly as a symbol of his dominance over a bovine electorate, possibly because he likes the taste of it.

Then there are snails. These look like snails, and to add insult to injury are usually served in their own homes. Like the ortolan (see below, §7), the snail goes through a purging process, being fed various cleansing ingredients for a few days (which seems a little strange, since any ingredients fed to a snail still turn to snail excrement), before being removed from their shells, killed, cooked, and replaced courteously in their shells with garlic and butter. Snails are naturally low in fat and high in protein, though if served in butter, the ratio is reversed.

Frogs' legs look like the legs of frogs, and taste of chicken. To kill and remove the legs from any animal – the killing is often simultaneous with, and caused by, the leg removal – and then blithely claim it tastes like another animal, is surely a terrible insult: a frog, if it could defend itself, would surely claim that it tastes like a frog. In recent years, at an archaeological dig at Amesbury in Wiltshire, a midden was uncovered containing hundreds of frog-leg bones dating back to the seventh millennium BC: the British are thus the original 'frogs'.

Or bone marrow. This is the 'meat butter' of beef or veal: it is cooked in the bone, which is longitudinally halved and garnished with mustard seeds, garlic and herbs, then served with garlic bread and salad. It's completely delicious – as long as you don't mind being reminded that you are eating an animal.

3.

Clink Glasses and Make Eye Contact

In France, when you clink glasses to toast one another, you are also supposed to look one another in the eye. Not to do so is to invite bad luck; it is also to demonstrate one's spiritual absence during this most important of encounters. After all, it is an encounter in which one traditionally wishes one's fellow drinker *bonne santé*, or 'good health'. Not to look them in the eye at this time is essentially to say: 'I care little for you or your health, or for this moment of fellowship between us; you don't really exist for me, and in fact you are trash, and I wouldn't visit you in hospital or attend your funeral, the date and circumstances of which are of no interest to me.'

Clinking is an interesting custom. Why do we clink? And why do the French clink more than the British? A Briton will often just raise his glass, look at nothing in particular, say 'cheers' and gulp it down. The French, on the other hand, love to clink.

Apparently it derives from a medieval custom. In former times it was quite possible that your host had poisoned your wine. In order to demonstrate that this was not so, the host would tip a portion of his wine into your glass (or beaker), and you would tip a portion of yours into his. The contact between the lips of the respective glasses or beakers as this was performed gave rise to the custom of clinking: rather than mix the wines together, one could symbolically clink as a mark of trust.

It would be amusing to pour one's wine into a Frenchman's wineglass these days and watch the expression on his face.

4.

Sample *Eau de Vie*

❋

Eau de vie means 'water of life', and derives ultimately from the Latin *aqua vitae* – which also found its way into Gaelic, giving us *uisge beatha*, literally 'water of life', or more familiarly, 'whiskey'.

Eau de vie is made from fermented fruit, which is then distilled. There is apple *eau de vie*, pear *eau de vie*, cherry *eau de vie*, raspberry *eau de vie*, and so on. It is usually clear, and is not aged, but drunk straight away (though if sealed with wax, it may be kept). Thus it has some affinities with *nouveau* wines: fresh, sprightly, straight from the bough or bush.

Eau de vie also holds an important place in French culture. Historically, producers of homemade spirituous liquors had the right to distil small quantities of *eau de vie* without being taxed: exemptions were granted for the distillation of 10 litres of pure alcohol or 20 litres of 50% alcohol. These stalwarts were known as *bouilleurs de cru*, or 'vineyard-boilers'.

Their privileges were hereditary until 1960, when, in an attempt to limit the scourge of alcoholism – and under pressure from major French producers and importers of alcohol – the legislature revoked hereditary rights. The situation worsened in 2008, when 50% taxes for the first ten litres of pure alcohol were imposed on surviving *bouilleurs*, after which 100% tax was payable.

Considering that most *bouilleurs* are pensioners and are dying off rapidly, these laws outraged rural communities and gave many French people the excuse, if any were needed, for undying hatred of all governments and their poxy interferences.

5.

Go to a Market

❋

The French market is not the pale phenomenon we are used to in the UK, with its worthy attempt to create a culture of 'local' producers in opposition to the dominance of the supermarket, which in reality has everything very nicely sewn up, thank you – it's a real tradition, alive in every French town and every French soul. *Le marché* is where once simultaneously tastes, smells, hears, feels and sees France. In this, it beats the most French of all other French things – a *sanisette*, a *baguette*, a *Catherinette* – into a cocked hat.

Markets are generally held once a week in most towns, though in some cases twice a week or more. The largest markets are special concerns known as *foires* (fairs) and take place on former religious occasions a few times a year. Covered markets (*marchés couverts*) also exist on a permanent basis, with stallholders specializing in every conceivable commodity (clothes, pictures, cheeses, olives, eggs, potatoes, honey, hats, pottery, tools, wine, flowers, books, chicks).

Some markets have a national fame: among them are the book market at Parc George Brassens in Paris, the flower market in Nice, the contemporary art market at Place de la Bastille in Paris, the fish market at Marseilles, the flea market at Place Saint Sulpice in Paris, and the stamp market at Avenue de Marigny in Paris.

The French love to browse, to prod, to finger, to disparage and finally to buy. And at noon everyone packs up for a long lunch, hypnotizing themselves with food and wine into a deep and endless afternoon.

6.

Eat Horse – on Purpose

⚙

In Britain we eat a lot of horse, but call it by another name: 'beef'.

In France they eat it deliberately. French horse-eating is not actually as widespread as the British like to make out – certainly not as widespread as it is in Kazakhstan or the Philippines – but the accusation of horse-eating is an important 'othering' tactic. The French eat horse, therefore they are monsters.

The French taste for horse is actually of fairly recent date. It goes back to the Revolution (1789), when commoners seized the mounts of the aristocracy and ate them out of spite. Later, in the Napoleonic wars, horse-eating became a battlefield necessity, and the French, being French, invented several new recipes to go with it, including some exciting new sauces. And in the Prussian siege of Paris in 1870, horse again appeared on the menu, along with all the animals of the Paris zoo. Once you've got a taste for sloth, it's difficult to go back to chicken.

On the British hypocrisy over horse: what many people may not appreciate is that even though the British don't, on the whole, eat horse on purpose, they do participate in the horseflesh trade. For example, New Forest ponies. Only around 50 stallions are required for stud work in the New Forest, and the remainder of the colts born – many hundreds a year – are slaughtered in the UK and dispatched on hooks to people on the Continent who will appreciate them.

7.

Eat an Ortolan

✳

An ortolan bunting is a small bird 'about the size of a young girl's fist' with a rather special place in French gastronomy. Ortolans used to be a delicacy, and were trapped every year by the hundreds of thousands, until they became an endangered species. In 1999, trapping, cooking or eating an ortolan was made illegal, on penalty of a €6,000 fine.

Ortolan-eating is surrounded by ritual. First of all, the bird is captured alive and force-fed millet in a dark box. Then it is drowned in Armagnac. Then it is plucked. Then, with its legs and head intact, it is roasted for a few minutes in a cassoulet until it begins to sizzle in its own yellow fat. Then it is eaten whole, innards and all.

The fun doesn't stop there. Traditionally, the diner places a napkin over his head while he eats the bird. This may be to concentrate ortolan-aromas, or it may be to protect the diner from the gaze of God, who would surely disapprove of a) the egregious sensuality of the practice, b) the egregious cruelty of the practice, or c) the egregious egregiousness of the practice.

An ortolan was the last meal of French president François Mitterrand in 1996: he died ten days afterwards, still possibly savouring the taste of the bird's flesh, the Armagnac pop of its tiny lungs, and the hazelnut crunch of its little skull.

Rumours persist that ortolan-eating has not been entirely eradicated. If you are in the south-west, have enough money and the right connections, then... *quelque chose est sans doute possible...*

8.

Ignore the French Paradox

❋

'The French paradox' is the observation that French people typically consume higher than average amounts of saturated fats, which are strongly associated with coronary heart disease, yet suffer from substantially lower rates of said coronary heart disease. In very rough terms, the French consume about 25% more saturated fats (in the form of soft cheeses, butter and fatty meat) than the Americans or British, but suffer from about 25% less heart disease.

When this was first noticed in the 1980s, there was a frenzy of interest throughout the world in exactly how the French were getting away with it. In America, it was claimed that the prophylactic factor was red wine. The US consumption of red wine quadrupled overnight, as Americans forced themselves to drink the filthy stuff as a health food. Vitamin K2 was also implicated (the only vitamin named after a mountain), since K2 can be found in

Brie de Meaux and *foie gras*. Other explanations involved smaller portion sizes, statistical incompetence, low sugar intake, herbal tea, not eating while watching TV, smoking plenty of cigarettes and saying 'ooh la la' occasionally. In fact, it was open season for anyone who wanted to write a book giving the reasons why French women don't get fat, old, ugly or develop varicose veins, and later, why French children don't have tantrums and why everyone in France is having so many orgasms that it is surprising their features are not twisted into a permanent rictus of ecstasy.

The only people who don't care about the French paradox are the French themselves, who have nothing to gain from finding out why, or indeed if, it exists.

9.

Become a Temporary Monarchist

The French, as we know, are prominent regicides. Yet one of their most cherished delicacies is the *galette des rois*, or 'cake of the kings'.

This is eaten at any time from Epiphany to the beginning of Lent. (Epiphany is the festival held on the 6th of January, when the Three Kings, aka the Three Wise Men, visited the baby Jesus.)

The *galette* is a round flaky pastry creation filled, usually, with frangipane, but also with chocolate, candied peel, figs or anything sweet and exotic. The consumption of the *galette* is hedged about by hundreds of years of tradition: according to this, the *galette* should be divided among the members of the household, with a final slice left over for the first beggar to approach the house. This final slice is known as the *part du pauvre* (poor man's slice), the *part du Bon Dieu* (the slice of the good Lord) or the *part de la Vierge* (the Virgin's slice). Entombed in the frangipane is a small trinket known as a *fève*, traditionally in the form of one of the figures of the Nativity, though now more often in the form of one of the figures of Disney. The person who gets the slice containing the *fève* is entitled to be king or queen for the day, and choose their consort.

Every year an enormous metre-wide *galette* is made for the President of the Republic and presented at the Elysée Palace with much fanfare. However, the Presidential *galette* does not include a *fève*. With a little reflection, it's easy to see why. If the president got a *fève* in his slice, he would become king for a day. Which would necessitate his immediate decapitation.

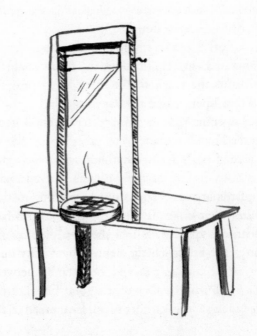

10.

Enjoy *L'heure de l'Apéro*

❀

L'heure de l'apéro is 'Apero Hour' or 'the hour of the aperitif'. *Apéritif* becomes *apéro* as *intellectuel* becomes *intello*, *vétérinaire* becomes *véto* and *hôpital* becomes hô*sto* – see §78.

What does *apéritif* mean, at its root? Well, it comes from the Latin verb *aperire*, to open, which also gives us the name of the month of April (the month that 'opens' the way to spring). The *apéritif* is thus the opening move in the protracted chess-game that is the French dinner.

However, an *apéro* is not something that you gulp back quickly before tucking in. The French, with their customary attention to the pleasures of the body, and their understanding of the way anticipation sharpens appetite in a variety of contexts, have elongated the act of having a snifter into sixty minutes. *L'heure de l'apéro* is the time spent between knocking off work (or, at weekends, recovering from a long lunch) and starting the evening meal. It is a time taken with friends at a café, riverbank, bar, etc., quite separate from the time taken at the restaurant or home where you will later dine. It is a prequel, but in a different cinema.

L'heure de l'apéro is an hour the French have created and demarcated for themselves, and is consequently an hour in which they feel the most French; so they may take the opportunity to re-make the world (see §43) or indulge in a few *contrepèteries* (see §84). There isn't really any English equivalent to *l'heure de l'apéro*. 'Having a pint with your mates after work' doesn't cut it.

The actual *apéro* in question could be anything – a glass of rosé, a cocktail, a pastis, etc. – which you could, though it is not usual, refer to as a *roso, cockto* or *pasto*.

11.

Eat at McDo's

Naturally, one would not wish to disparage McDonald's fine products or suggest that *une McBaguette* is anything but delicious and nutritious: but it comes as rather a surprise to learn that the French, lovers of *haute cuisine* in all its forms, enthusiastic ingesters of calf's head and snails, have more McDonald's restaurants than the UK, and are in fact in sixth position in the world for proximity of a McDonald's, after the USA, Japan, China, Germany and Canada.

It's a growing phenomenon. Not just McDonald's: Burger King, which tried to penetrate the French market in the late 90s but was forced to withdraw in flaccid ignominy, opened its first new franchise at the Gare Saint Lazare in 2014, and apparently has plans to expand aggressively into McDonald's French demesnes.

How could this be? France is as protective of its food culture as it is of its language. A recent law called the *fait maison*, or 'made at home' law, made it compulsory for restaurants to stipulate exactly how each dish on their menu is prepared, precisely so as to reduce the volume of processed foods going down French gullets.

One possible reason is that the French love meat. Vegetarianism is not popular. There are less than half the number of self-confessed vegetarians in France as there are in the UK. And the market for burgers is not confined to fast-food outlets. Whereas around a billion fast-food burgers were sold in France in 2013, around half that number again were sold in sit-down restaurants. The growth in burger sales is actually partly fuelled by traditional dining habits: people are happy to order an artisanal burger in a chic restaurant, and having acquired the taste for it, go on to the hard stuff.

French Attitudes

12.

Don't talk about money: it's tacky

French people would prefer to talk about anything other than money. For example, they'd prefer to talk about sex, though perhaps this will not come as a great surprise.

When socializing with French people, bringing up the subject of money, salaries, investments, etc. is in very poor taste. For several reasons. Firstly, it goes against the French fantasy that the truest values in life are personal, philosophical and cultural. The French are happy to talk about the latest auction price of a Modigliani, but revealing the price of their new TV set would be bourgeois in the extreme. Secondly, to suggest that anyone earns more than anyone else is to run counter to the strong strain of egalitarianism in the French mindset (*liberté, egalité, fraternité*). Thirdly, there is a fear of the taxman, who might be listening anywhere: perhaps in the TV. Fourthly, there is a fear of exciting hostility and envy.

Some commentators ascribe this to the former peasant culture in which every pigherd kept a stash of coins at home: talking about exactly which pig the stash was located under would be asking for trouble.

In 2011 a scandal occurred in a subsidiary of the French IT company Capgemini: all the employees received an email, by mistake, showing exactly how much their colleagues earned. It caused social meltdown. The management pretended to re-jig all salaries to re-establish public amnesia: and everyone pretended to ignore the fact that their own salary hadn't changed.

13.

Pour scorn on everything

In France, the default attitude is negative.

> USA: Where's the John?
> UK: Sorry to bother you, but if it's not too much trouble could you possibly tell me whereabouts I can find the loo?
> France: The facilities here are not very well signposted, are they?

In France, conveniences are always inconvenient. But being negative is not just miserabilism.

Let's say you present a French friend with your new business plan for opening a cake shop. Your friend will tell you that there is not enough walk-by traffic, that taxes are too high, that no one eats cake any more. Cake! What a foolish idea! I scoff at your cake!

Of course they will say this: they're your friend.

Why would they tell you that everything will be fine? They'd only do that to an idiot or someone they didn't respect.

And your friend might also be trying to present themselves in a good light, as a canny advisor and a human being worthy of respect. The French have a fear of appearing naïve, innocent, lacking in *savoir-faire*. They know that people are selfish, the future is uncertain, the world is full of hazards, and that pride comes before a fall. Pointing out the deficiencies of anything is a way of demonstrating you understand the true clockwork of the universe.

14.

Bash France

The true clockwork of the universe also involves pointing out that France itself is irremediably flawed.

This may come as a surprise to anyone who knows any French people, who seem, at least on the surface, to value their *boulangeries* and the heroes of their Panthéon (see §56). That's probably because France-bashing is a sport that the French only indulge in when they are with their own kind. And once they really get going, tearing into France's perennial labour disputes, political skulduggery, pension reforms, factory closures, immigration problems, etc., they are in a class of their own, certainly way ahead of the British. Whereas a Briton will cheerfully admit that the UK is going to hell in a handcart, and pass from the topic to something more interesting, a Frenchman will settle in for a viciously detailed autopsy of the bloated corpse of the Fifth Republic.

A poll taken by the France 24 TV station during the fag-end of the Iraq War found that 44 percent of French people had a negative view of France, as opposed to 38 percent of Americans. Thus, at a time when American disdain for the French was at its height, it was clear that the French hated themselves more than the Americans did. *You think you hate us? Pah. You are mere beginners.*

This is anti-Chauvinism, in the original meaning of the word. Perhaps Chauvinism is a myth, and never really existed. Historians have been unable to demonstrate that such a person as Nicolas Chauvin, the supposed super-patriotic soldier in Napoleon's army, ever breathed. This seems highly symbolic: at the root of French pride and self-identification is a void of existential uncertainty.

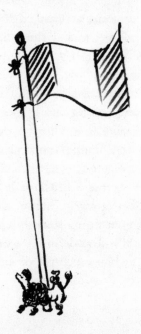

15.

Be Enormously Arrogant

What is French anti-Chauvinism and anti-patriotism? Take the question to any psychologist worth their salt and they will tell you: the flip-side of a superiority complex. The French know they are the best, and because of that very fact can't endure falling short. They complain in order to demonstrate that they have high standards.

As it happens, France is not a bad place to live. It has a skilled workforce, fast trains, lots of nice infrastructure that really works, and more broadband penetration than Germany (and Germany is very penetrated in this respect). It is the second-largest economy in Europe and the fifth-largest in the world by nominal GDP. It ranks number four in terms of attracting foreign capital, and – a crucial statistic – is the world's sixth-largest *exporter* of goods. Most of its frogs'-legs are imported, but a country can only breed so many frogs. On which subject, the birth-rate in France is climbing steadily, and has just topped two children per woman, which is, by the standards of industrialized Western nations, pretty high (compare e.g. Portugal at 1.5, Germany at 1.4 and Poland at 1.3). If the French really do see nothing in the future but decline and misery, would they be reproducing with such élan?

Another impressive statistic: France is the world's leading tourist destination. More people want to come to France for a holiday than to Greece, China, the USA... and the reason is not hard to find. The French really do seem to know how to live. They revel in food, sex, love, fashion and good conversation.

Perhaps the situation could be summarized thus: at heart, the French believe that societies are perfectible. Shangri-la is just around the corner. All that needs to happen to bring it into being is a little more moaning.

16.

Be Pragmatic

❁

The French, as has been mentioned, fear the darker side of life. They are more depressed than other European nations (see §40). They tend to be more negative (§13) and they habitually employ understatement (§75), preferring to tell you that something is not horrible rather than that it is good – which goes to show that what is horrible is what is expected.

There is, however, an upside to all of this. The French, grounded in their realistic view of life's terrors, are by that very fact better equipped to take steps to mitigate those terrors.

People get awful diseases and die. True, says the French person. So let's build a good health service. It's the least we can do while we are hanging around deteriorating. Or: travel is boring and time-consuming. It's just one of the depressing facts of life. So why not do something like create a network of high-speed trains. That at least would help in some small way to compensate for the absurdity of life and the futility of wanting to get from A to B anyway.

The French are a practical people. They recognise that there is much that is outside human control. The big events of life, the things that really matter, who you love, who loves you, how many of them there are, what positions they do it in, etc., are accidents of birth and chance. Life is unpredictable and complex. In the limited field of endeavour governed by the individual will, one simply does one's best with what one has.

17.

Reject the Bourgeois Institution of Marriage

Who calls it a bourgeois institution? Why, Ségolène Royal, Socialist government minister, who lived unwed with François Hollande, France's President, for 29 years, and bore him four children. Living in unwed bliss (or misery) is now completely normalized for the French. They are among the most unwed people in Europe. The crude marriage rate for France (crude marriage is not something you do with raw carrots in the privacy of your own home, but the number of marriages per year for every 1,000 inhabitants) was 3.7 in 2011, as compared to Britain at 4.5 and Sweden at 5.0. Among European nations, only a scant few are lower (Hungary sweeps the board as the most unwed nation at 2.9 per 1,000).

Why is this? It's nothing to do, as we in Britain might imagine, with single mothers and sink estates. It's an attitudinal change. Young French people increasingly reject the Catholic Church, the bourgeois (à la Ségolène) values of their parents, the patriarchal taint of the marriage vows, and the sheer pointlessness of it all. One can do all the things one can do in marriage – buy a house, have children and devote one's evenings to sullen silences – without being married. And if one wants to enshrine certain rights and responsibilities in a legal manner, there is the PACS, or *pacte civil de solidarité*, the French version of the civil partnership, which has been available to both homosexual and heterosexual couples since 1999.

In the past, people got married because it was impossible to imagine not getting married. Now, there is a recognition that when two people love each other, society doesn't have to come into it. And here, as always for the French, lies the nub of it. What does the Athens of the State have to do with the Jerusalem of the Heart? Once one grants true sovereignty to the individual, all other authorities tend to wither away.

18.

Espouse *Laïcité*

※

In the UK, our politicians 'don't do God'. We don't have any particular laws about not doing it: we just don't do it. Perhaps we find it embarrassing.

In France, things are different. Secularism, or as they term it, *laïcité*, is a central plank of public life, and enshrined in law. Article 1 of the Constitution magnificently declares that *La France est une République indivisible, laïque, démocratique et sociale*. And in 1905 a law was passed formally separating Church and State, which forbade any religious interference in public life and any government interference in religious life. It also, rather paradoxically, appropriated all religious buildings to local council authorities.

This was further reinforced in 2007, when a ban was imposed on the wearing of religious insignia such as Stars of David, Sikh turbans or large crucifixes in schools; and in 2011, by the banning of face-coverings in public, which effectively outlawed the *burqa* and *niqab*. This followed an incident in 2010 when two *burqa*-clad felons robbed a post-office.

For the French, therefore, religion cannot be conducted in the public sphere and must remain a private affair. It joins that other matter, one's salary, in the most delicate region of social intercourse. In religion and money, the French respect and value discretion. As the saying goes, *Pour vivre heureux, vivons cachés* ('to live happily, live hidden').

Christine Boutin, the leader of the *Parti Chrétien-démocrate*, a conservative Christian party, who looks not unlike Dawn French in *The Vicar of Dibley*, is well known for fulminating against same-sex marriage and abortion, and once famously did so while holding a Bible. The tactic was widely ridiculed.

19.

Be Serious about Privacy

When it comes to privacy, there are real and important differences between France and the UK. French privacy legislation is tough, and anyone flouting the law risks a heavy fine and/or imprisonment. Article 9 of the Civil Code sets out that 'everyone has the right to respect for his or her private life', and this private life is interpreted as including almost anything that a person gets up to while not discharging his or her public duties: making love, pursuing hobbies and interests, taking part in politics or trade union activity, worshipping God, going to the doctor, spending time with family and friends, etc. There are also tough laws on photographs (and drawings) of people: here the relevant articles are 226-1 to 226-9 of the Penal Code, amended in 1994 to curb the antics of the paparazzi, which make it illegal to capture another person's image in any private place without their consent, regardless of whether or not it is later disseminated. In the French legal system it also doesn't matter whether you are living or dead, since the privacy law extends beyond the grave.

All this has meant that some matters very central to French political life have been hushed up. Mitterrand's illegitimate daughter was known to the media for twenty years but managed to remain a secret. Neither were the press unaware of Chirac's many mistresses. Things are changing, slowly: magazines are emerging that are willing to take greater risks, but there is still an awareness that fines could be prohibitive.

Damages are awarded not in such a way as to address the heinous nature of the intrusion, as in Anglo-Saxon law, but the degree of trauma suffered by the victim. Thus if you can prove that you suffered very greatly over a minor revelation – say about the existence of a small rash – you can potentially reap greater damages than if you were revealed to be conducting an affair, if it can be shown that conducting the affair was merely an itch you had to scratch.

20.

Disparage the Regions

Of course, what counts as a 'region' depends where you start from. Recently a series of highly amusing maps was drawn up by the website *Cartes France*. These show France as perceived by its various inhabitants. So, for example, from the point of view of Paris, Brittany to the west is the realm of *alcooliques* (alcoholics), the Pas de Calais is inhabited by *pauvres* (the poor), the Alsace region to the east by *dépressifs* (the depressed), and the southern half of the country (particularly Marseilles) by *branleurs* (tossers) and *menteurs* (liars). If you are from Marseilles, on the other hand, then Paris is a zone of *cons* (arseholes) and Normandy is so far north as to be populated by Esquimaux. The same map as perceived by the residents of Normandy shows most of the rest of the country as *vaches concurrentes* (cow-breeding competitors) and Parisians as *envahisseurs du weekend* (weekend invaders).

French identity is multiple. Of course, UK citizens too have multiple identities: the inhabitants of Newcastle are first and foremost Geordies, then English, then Europeans. But in France, regional pride tends to be stronger even than that encountered on the banks of the Tyne. This is partly because France is more linguistically diverse than the UK. In the French regions, people don't just speak their own dialects, but in some cases their own separate languages, such as Alsatian, Breton and Occitan (see §88). And along with separate languages, of course, go separate cultural practices, cuisines etc. A Breton might see himself or herself as almost a different species from an Alsatian (no pun intended).

In Britain we are used to this debate about identity, of course, but usually in the context of recent immigration. France has both recent immigration and ancient regional demarcations to worry about, leading to a much greater volume of day-to-day discussion on the real meaning of Frenchness.

21.

Worship Intellectuals

In Britain it is impossible to apply the word 'intellectual' to any thinker, writer or commentator without an undercurrent of abuse: the implication is that the person in question is slightly absurd, not a little pretentious, and lives in an ivory tower with his ten mistresses. In France, of course, there is no problem: mistresses are an indispensable part of life and there can never be enough elephants to satisfy the demand for ivory towers.

From the *philosophes* (Voltaire, Diderot, Rousseau) onward, through Saussure and Bergson, to Sartre, Camus and de Beauvoir, and in the post-modern era Barthes, Lacan, Baudrillard and Bernard-Henri Lévy, the intellectual is at the heart of French culture. His role (it is usually a he) is to examine and question current dogmas and to demolish simplistic thinking. He may be a novelist, a social theorist, a critic or merely someone sitting in a café pontificating; he may be a rebel, a wastrel or an out-and-out self-satirist. One of the most respected French intellectuals of the later twentieth century, Gilles Deleuze, referred to his own critical method as 'buggery', since it involved reading the work of other writers in a manner never intended by those authors (for example treating Montesquieu as a feminist). French intellectuals delight in perversity. Georges Perec's famous work *La Disparition* is written entirely without the use of the letter 'e'. Some intellectuals even go to the extreme of claiming they are not responsible for their own literary output. This was the approach taken by the Emeritus Professor of Roman History at the University of Paris, Marcel Bénabou, in his ravishingly tongue-in-cheek *Pourquoi je n'ai écrit aucun de mes livres* ('Why I Have Not Written Any of My Books'), which was a huge hit in France and encouraged Bénabou to produce a follow-up, *Jette ce livre avant qu'il soit trop tard* ('Dump This Book While You Still Can'), which pleads with its readers: 'Come on, dump this book. Or better yet, throw it as far away as you can. Right now. Before it's too late. That resolution is your only escape, believe me.'

22.

Be a Sexist Pig

In a recent film by Éléonore Pourriat, *Majorité Opprimée* ('Oppressed Majority') a French man is shown at the receiving end of everyday sexist behaviour. He is repeatedly groped and leered at; bare-breasted women jog past him in the street where he pushes a stroller; and there is an extraordinary scene in which he argues nervously with a male friend who has decided to wear a headscarf. The film was intended as a satire, of course.

Many French women feel that their menfolk are among the most unregenerate sexists in the world. The problem seems particularly ingrained in political life. One recent *cause célèbre* was 'Poulegate': this occurred when a male MP in the *Assemblée Nationale*, seemingly the worse for wear, repeatedly barracked a female speaker who was attempting an entirely reasonable speech on pension reform, by making clucking noises. The noises were intended to indicate that she was a *poule*, which, in French, implies she is a brainless floozie. The next day several female members of the *Assemblée* staged a protest by arriving late for the session; an outraged group of male MPs then retaliated by staging a walkout.

Then there is the DSK situation. Dominique Strauss-Kahn was the director of the International Monetary Fund who was arrested in 2011 when a hotel chambermaid accused him of sexual assault. The case was thrown out when witness testimony was shown to be unreliable, but the affair polarized opinion. The essential pro-DSK script was supplied by former French Minister of Culture, Jack Lang, who said: 'No one is dead.'

French Behaviour

23.

Exchange Kisses

The British are mightily confused by Latin kissing behaviour. British people don't have body language, any more than De Gaulle had a hamster. For the British, public body contact is embarrassing and un-necessary. And erotic. Obviously kissing has something to do with sex.

In French, to kiss on meeting or parting is *faire la bise*. A kiss on each cheek is exchanged, with perhaps a third on the first cheek, and then, for really devoted practitioners bubbling with *joie de vivre*, a fourth on the second cheek. The number of kisses is often a matter of region: in Nîmes, for example, it's three kisses, and in Marseilles, two. There is also a 'neutral' position of two kisses taken by the French abroad.

Latin kissing behaviour signifies a happy and relaxed desire for intimacy and friendship. It express-es the power of women, since they can kiss who they like, including children, and demonstrates the relatively fluid and polyglot nature of female sexuality. Men can kiss too, but heterosexual men may have to be a little more careful when kissing other heterosexual men, if they don't want to send out the message: 'I desire a *ménage à trois* with you and another man and perhaps a fourth man, at my place, now.'

If you are British you will make a hideous mess of this, but no French person expects anything more of you.

24.

Pisser dans la Rue

⁂

A fairly self-explanatory activity, this is common in France, particularly in the big cities. Men relieve themselves against walls, under bridges, on stairs, or even in the métro, though not usually on the live rail. Perhaps the French celebration of the body is responsible. Specifically the male body.

The authorities in Paris, who are forced to spend millions of euros trying to dam the tides of urine (Rabelais would have laughed), have opened hundreds of modern *sanisettes*, or unisex toilets. These are ignored, sometimes by men actually pissing up against their sides.

Then there's the anti-pissing wall, or *mur anti-pipi*, invented by one Etienne Vanderpooten: this is ridged in such a way that it sprays your own urine back at you, leaving you with comically spattered shoes. It is, Mr Vanderpooten says, a case of the '*arroseur arrosé*' (the sprinkler sprinkled).

But France has many walls, and they can't all be booby-trapped.

For the hordes of urine criminals, a special squad called the *Brigade des Incivilités* has the power to hand out on-the-spot court orders. The official offence is *miction sur la voie publique*, and offenders can, if convicted, face up to a €450 fine. But the *Brigade* is unable to levy on-the-spot fines. Thus, tourists and the homeless, or anyone else without an address, has a free urination pass.

25.

Make French Gestures

✸

The French are masters of the gesture. The Gallic shrug is perhaps the best known, shoulders up, hands out, palm upwards, and lower lip protruding, as if to say: 'What can you do?', 'It's the way of the world', 'It's not my responsibility', 'Do I look like I give a damn?', 'So he died, it happens to everyone', etc. The meanings are subtle and infinite. It may be accompanied by the sound '*Bof*'.

Another gesture, and one that is easily misinterpreted, because a similar gesture exists in the English-speaking world, is when a French person passes his hand, palm-down, over his head. This doesn't mean 'It's over my head' or 'I didn't understand it' but 'That's it. I've taken enough of this *merde*.' It's often paired with the phrases *j'en ai ras le bol* ('I've had a bowl-ful') or *j'en ai ras la casquette* ('I've had a hat-ful').

Another French gesture that is hard to interpret,

or personally master, is the limp hand-flap. This is performed by holding the hand in the region of your stomach and shaking it as if your fingers are hot; it may be accompanied by an outbreath or whistle, or the phrase *ooh la la*. It usually signifies a species of emotional overload. It can mean that someone is very skilled at something, or very sexy; it can signify that something was painful, brutal or astonishing. In extreme cases the double hand flap is used.

Since the French regard gestures as an essential adjunct to speech, they deserve two entries.

26.

Make More French Gestures

Another you will see and be flummoxed by, is a gesture that looks like the French person is sticking two fingers up at you – only in this case the two fingers are going up the nose, or at least are dangerously close to doing so. This means 'It's easy' or 'It's a piece of cake,' and may be accompanied by the words '*Les doigts dans le nez.*' Example situation: you are taking part in the Tour de France. How to get ahead? Your French friend sticks two fingers up his nose. '*Les doigts dans le nez*', he says. 'You must simply spread grease over the road by that hairpin bend and watch them all tumble into the ravine.'

Then there is the *barrons-nous* gesture. This consists of holding both hands in front of you, palm down, and slapping one hand on top of the other rather as if you were giving yourself a playful 'slap on the wrist'. What it means, however, is 'Let's split' or 'Let's get the hell out of here.' As such it is a gesture that requires to be performed in some secrecy, since if your hostess notices you making it, she will be offended and will wonder if her ortolan was up to scratch.

Sometimes French gestures do seem to have a secretive or 'thieves parlance' aspect to them – that is, they communicate something privately that might be offensive if said aloud. An example of this is the *Il a un verre dans le nez* ('He has a glass in his nose') gesture. This indicates that someone is drunk. In this, you hold your fist in front of your nose and twist it, rotating your head in the other direction. Sounds difficult – and actually is.

A final 'secret-offensive' gesture, maybe now not so often seen, is *Il a un poil dans la main* ('He has a hair in his hand'). This indicates that someone is lazy. To perform it, you mime plucking a hair from your palm. Presumably the person concerned does so little work that hairs can grow freely on this surface. In the case of extremely lazy persons, *Il a un baobab dans la main* may be used.

27

Make French Noises

The French make all sorts of extra-linguistic utterances, interjections and ejaculations. Here are four:

1. **A sort of gasp** or quick vocalized breath in, almost as if signifying shock. In French, however, it signifies agreement and fellow-feeling. If you say, for example, 'It really should be illegal to piss against the wall of the primary school' – you will get the sharp vocalized gasp plus a comment – 'True. Although I think it is, actually.'

2. **A fart-sound** made with the lips. A real raspberry sound. This is where your auditor has given up on understanding you, your question, life, and has no interest in any further intercourse with you. Basically it means: 'I have no idea.' Example: 'Do you know where I can get an ortolan? The President is coming to dinner.' [Auditor makes a raspberry sound to signify that they don't know and have no interest in helping you.]

3. **The sound '*hop!*'** This occurs in the well-known French utterance '*Allez hop!*', though it also exists on its own. It is a small expression of satisfaction at having done something with dispatch and precision, such as putting a child on a high shelf. It can also mean 'move along!' or 'let's go!' and may be paired with a small bounce on one's heels.

4. **A growl** to signify frustration. This is made at the back of the throat as if trying to dislodge a fish-bone, or the scapula of an ortolan. Where a British person might give vent to an 'aaargh', the French utterance in the same situation is right back in the throat and doesn't involve the larynx: it's a vibration of the tonsils. Example: 'Damn, the buses are on strike again! [Growl]. Now I can't go mushroom-picking.'

28.

Faire le Pont

❉

The French cherish their public holidays: the nationally-recognised ones comprise New Year's Day, Easter Monday, Labour Day/May Day, Victory in Europe Day, Ascension, Whit Monday, Bastille Day, Assumption, All Saints' Day, Armistice Day and Christmas Day, with others in the regions. Sometimes these holidays fall on Tuesdays or Thursdays, and in these cases the French *font le pont*, or 'make the bridge', to form a long weekend, i.e. Saturday-Sunday-Monday-Tuesday or Thursday-Friday-Saturday-Sunday. Businesses may close or work half days on the extra Monday or Friday, and small family-run businesses may close for the entire term.

Of course, in the UK, public holidays are engineered to fall perennially on a Monday, which, now one looks at it, is a transparent means by which the ruling classes seek to stop ordinary people from exercising their right to bunk off.

Which leaves the problem, for the French, of what to do if the holiday falls on a Wednesday. Taking two days off to *faire le pont* is quite outrageous, naturally, but when the boldest of practitioners attempt it, it is known not as *faire le pont*, but *faire le viaduc*.

Naturally one can *faire le viaduc* either side of a Wednesday, or conceivably both, resulting in a single public holiday that lasts nine days.

29.

Smoke Yourself to Death

The Anglophone world anathematizes smoking and the Francophone exalts it. This exaltation leads to the deaths of around 73,000 French citizens per year. But everyone has to go sometime, and passing up the pleasure of a cigarette just because you are afraid of a painful death is just not very French. You wouldn't have caught Simone de Beauvoir fretting over the pictures on a packet of *Gitanes*: she had more important things to worry about, such as who Jean-Paul Sartre was currently sharing a post-coital fag with.

In France, as elsewhere in Europe, it's illegal to smoke in public places; but because 30 percent of the population smoke, fewer people care if someone lights up in a forbidden zone. The result is that anti-smoking laws are widely flouted.

French cigarettes are actually quite heavily taxed, but it doesn't make any difference to smoking rates: in any case, people can get their cigarettes from

Belgium or other European countries, where tax is lower, and the allowance is fairly generous: ten cartons per person per trip. Or they can buy outright contraband. It's been estimated that around a quarter of all the cigarettes smoked in France are smuggled in illegally.

The issue is really one of culture and fashion. Coco Chanel smoked 50 a day and lived to be 87.

30.

Demonstrate

❀

The French are a conservative people. Now, this may seem a ludicrous thing to say in the face of French history, which is a welter of revolutions, uprisings, wars, demonstrations and strikes. But the two things go together. Change, for the French, is all or nothing. Big changes: OK, if it means getting rid of a corrupt king. Small changes that benefit individuals, or creeping change that threatens to erode traditional values: not OK. Therefore, when French people demonstrate, they most often demonstrate against change, not for it. Demonstrations against gay marriage laws; demonstrations against Islamicization; demonstrations against changes to the baccalaureate exam; demonstrations against pension reforms. As mentioned elsewhere, you will find it difficult to pin a French person down on what they are for, and much easier to pin them down on what they are against.

The Prefecture of Police licenses thousands of demonstrations every year in Paris, which is surprising given the fact that demonstrators are often actively hostile to the police. The main way the police get their revenge is by underestimating the number of people on the demonstration. Thus the organizers will say that 500,000 people came out to protest against the visit of a certain Shi'ite cleric; the police will say it was 350. The organizers will say the demonstration passed off peacefully: the police will say that each of those 350 torched two cars apiece.

In the film *Marathon Man*, which is set partly in Paris, a demonstration can be heard chanting in the background. Strangely enough, they are chanting in 5/4 time. It may only be in France that this is possible.

31.

Have your Strike and Eat It

The French have the reputation of being a nation of strikers. The French themselves take a rueful delight in drawing attention to this reputation. And it's true: there are more days lost to work per annum in France than almost anywhere else in the world (except Canada, which has a lot of French people).

But this is not the whole story. French strikes disproportionately affect the civil service and state-run industries, particularly transport. When it comes to the private sector, the French are restrained. It may also come as a surprise that very low numbers of French workers sign up to trade unions – only about 8%.

And despite the constant strikes, French productivity is very high by global standards. France's labour productivity, a measure of GDP per hour worked, was £36 at the last showing (OECD 2012 figures), a long way ahead of the UK at £29 and the average Euro-zone figure of £31. So it seems that the French can go on strike, then somehow work more efficiently than everyone else when they clock back on. It's essentially French Paradox Number Two (see above, §8).

Why are the French so keen to draw attention to this 'French disease' of incessant strikes? The French wish to believe that they are simultaneously the best and the worst nation in the world, and if they are uniquely paralysed by strikes, it's a negative distinction, if nothing else.

32.

Work Less than Everyone Else

❁

Are the French lazy? Not at all. They are merely clever. The French have achieved a better work/life balance than most other countries in the world.

According to the OECD, the French work 1,479 hours per person per year. Only some Scandinavian countries and Germany work less than that. In Italy, they work 1,752 hours; in the Czech Republic, 1,784; in Poland, 1,929; and in Chile, 2,029. But a comparison of the labour productivity in these countries with the hours actually worked is instructive: in France, for each of those 1,479 hours, they garner £36. In Italy, for 1,752, they garner £27. In the Czech Republic, for 1,784, they garner £18. In Poland, for 1,929, £16. And in Chile, for 2,029, £15. It's a law of diminishing returns, and the French seem to have pitched it just right.

The low number of hours worked by the average French person is partly a legacy of French politics.

In the early 2000s the left-wing government of Lionel Jospin introduced a 35-hour working week in order to spread work more evenly among the population and reduce unemployment. (This has now largely been eroded by successive governments, but the 35-hour week remains a shibboleth of left-right battles.) Jospin's other stated aim was to take advantage of France's prosperity to give French people a better quality of life. In other words, what was really at stake was Gross Domestic Pleasure. The people should have the leisure to reward themselves for their labours, to take holidays in the country, and to ingest goodly quantities of foods that in other countries would lead to rapid death from cardiac disease, but somehow, in France, don't.

Never has the Protestant work ethic seemed so hollow.

33.

Jump the Queue

✺

Actually the French word *queue* – and it is a French word – is an interesting one. It means a tail, and when it was first borrowed into English it meant a pigtail of hair. It was only later that the word was adapted metaphorically to mean 'a line of people'. Before around 1850, if you formed a queue, you plaited your hair.

French queues are somewhat fluid. Not as fluid as they are in Italy or China, but fluid nevertheless. For example, a queue of people might be waiting for a coach. The coach arrives. Suddenly the activity is no longer waiting for a coach. It is playing rugby.

Or you are waiting in line at a cheesemonger. The cheesemonger is about to close, and the next three days are all holidays (see §28). There are eight people in the queue. Suddenly an old lady hobbles to the front and asks for a small piece of Roquefort for her cat. She is served, and hobbles out. What just happened? Well, the old lady is a former comrade-in-arms of Abbé Pierre, the Resistance hero and Catholic priest. She is too old, and too *Parisiennne*, for things such as queues. The French people in the queue feel resentful but they understand it. The old lady isn't a cipher, a sheep, a herd animal. They aspire to be like her. They too despise petit-bourgeois edicts. One day they too will blow all this queuing nonsense out of the water and assert their true French individualism.

One final note: *queue* in French also means penis.

34.

Be Fifteen Minutes Late

Take the case of Nathalie and Jon. Nathalie is French and Jon is Swedish, and they are in love. Nathalie is a fashion buyer who works hard and has numerous clients. Jon is a software designer who works at home and rarely gets up before noon. It might be expected that Jon would be the one who is always late. In fact the problem lies with Nathalie. Jon waits around for her in cafés, bars at or his flat, getting increasingly angry.

The difficulty is one of culture. Nathalie hails from a culture in which it is actually polite to turn up late. Being fifteen or twenty minutes late for appointments is a courtesy, the reasoning goes, because it gives the person you are meeting time to settle themselves, relax and prepare for the encounter – and gives both parties a margin of error in case either is unavoidably delayed. In the case of attending a dinner party, it's even more vital, as it gives the hostess just a bit of extra time to make sure the table settings are perfect, the glasses are clean, and the armpits are shaved.

Jon, however, late-rising as he is, comes from a Nordic culture where courtesy is parcelled out in minutes. He can see that Nathalie is never late for work, and doesn't see why she can't behave the same way towards him. Nathalie, however is insulted that he would think that their relationship is in any sense 'work'.

Jon tells her that henceforward, more than five minutes late for a meeting with him and he will regard her as in breach of contract. Nathalie regards this as ridiculous.

Jon and Nathalie are no longer together. Nathalie is now with a nice Spanish man, Jorge. Unfortunately Jorge's habit of keeping her waiting for more than half an hour at lunch is beginning to get on her nerves.

35.

Address God as *Tu*

In French, you have a choice: you can address people either as *tu* or as *vous*. *Tu* is the singular form, and is informal and friendly; *vous* is the plural form, and is formal and respectful. In other words, if you want to be polite in France, you pretend that there is more than one of the person you are talking to.

Students address teachers as *vous*; the teacher may then respond with a *tu*, or perhaps with a *vous* if they wish to show equal respect. People address their dogs as *tu*, though the dogs do not usually respond. Interviewers address their interviewees with *vous*. Young children address their parents with *tu*, except in families where beatings are common. God is addressed as *tu*, to show that he is a loving father, and not about to administer a beating – though he probably is.

Calling someone *tu* is known as *tutoiement*, and calling them *vous* as *vouvoiement*. It's a very subtle thing: to *tutoie* someone prematurely shows gaucheness, and may invite a put-down. A famous instance occurred when François Mitterrand was asked by a supporter: 'On se tutoie?' ('Is it OK to use tu?'). Mitterrand glacially replied: 'Comme vous voulez.' ('As you wish').

This exchange shows that the use of *vous* does not involve merely the expression of respect. It may also show hauteur. Similarly with *tu*. For example, you might think it would be normal to 'talk down' to a maid in a hotel, using *tu*. But this would be in very bad taste, showing you were lacking a proper spirit of *égalité*.

Perhaps this was the problem in a certain recent political scandal. He *tutoied* the maid, and then things got out of hand.

36.

Stare Unapologetically at People

✹

The French, and particularly Parisians, will stare at you as if you represent a challenging ethnographic puzzle. The stare seems to say: 'All around me are human beings. But look, a funny little monkey has joined us. How comical, in a very serious way, that she thinks she can wear shoes.'

That is what the stare seems to say. In fact it is saying something quite different. It really means: 'Ah, look, a fellow human being. She doesn't care that she is absurd, just like the rest of us. How comical, in a very serious way, that she thinks she can wear shoes.'

In France, this sort of frank staring is most often encountered outside cafés, where French people sit because the fumes are pleasant. The outside of a café is a curious zone. It is neither inside nor properly outside. It is what psychologists and anthropologists call a 'liminal' zone: a threshold, a borderland, neither one thing nor the other. In accord with this liminality, people sitting on café pavements look both outward at the passing pedestrian traffic, and inward at waiters and refreshments. But if they enjoy observing the passing scene, then they too are being carefully scrutinized, and, in fact, preyed upon: they are an impromptu audience, ripe for exploitation by street musicians and other suppliers of dubious entertainment.

When people stare at you in France, just stare back. Breathtakingly, it won't get you beaten up.

French Well-Being

37

Try Thalassotherapy

Thalassotherapy is the use of seawater, sea mud, seaweed, algae and other seaside exudations to promote health. It became popular in Brittany in the 19th century and remains popular in France today. Of course, the use of the sea as a therapy is common to all cultures, and anyone who goes in for a dip in freezing rollers and comes out with a warm glow has just taken part in a thalassotherapeutic session; but the French have elevated it into something of an art.

Thalassotherapists will naturally claim that the minerals found in seawater, seaweed, algae, etc. – potassium, magnesium, sodium, calcium, iodine – can cure a long list of distressing conditions, from athlete's foot to schizophrenia. There doesn't seem to be much evidence to support this, but French people flock to *thalasso* centres anyway, in defiance of medical opinion. Conventional doctors are OK for getting antibiotics and contraception, but when you really need to breathe in some sea-fog to help you with the pins and needles you occasionally get after a long lunch, where are they?

Thalasso centres need not necessarily be on the coast. They could be in the arid heart of the Bouches du Rhône or on top of a mountain in the Massif Centrale. The entrepreneurs who run *thalasso* spas are adept at collecting the fruits of the ocean and transporting them to wherever clients most need to coat themselves in mud and barnacles.

38.

See a *Rebouteux*

In the deepest darkest depths of rural France, witches still live. These people are known as *rebouteux* (no adequate translation exists – 'bonesetters' might be a rough equivalent) or *coupeurs de feu* ('fire cutters'). They exist to service the needs of ordinary people with trapped nerves, bad backs or nasty shooting pains down one side, people who have been failed by doctors and the State. Ah, the State. The French hate it so profoundly.

The existence of these *rebouteux* was brought to light by a recent film, *Mon âme par toi guérie*, or 'You Healed My Soul', directed by François Dupeyron. The film follows the life of Fredi, a reluctant trailer-trash healer who has inherited his powers from his mother, and who brings a boy back from the brink of death after he, Fredi, has run him over with his motorbike.

Naturally the actual mechanism by which this

healing art operates is difficult to delimit. The French confraternity of alternative practitioners, known by the wonderful acronym GNOMA (*Groupement national pour l'organisation des médecines alternatives*), ascribe it to magnetism, or perhaps to the manipulation of certain energy meridians, or perhaps to powers that lie beyond rational analysis. All that is certain is that a true *rebouteux* or *rebouteuse* can be recognised by this simple test: if, after taking an organic orange or lemon in his or her hands for ten minutes every day for ten days, the fruit becomes as hard as a rock and is completely dry inside, the nascent *rebouteux* or *rebouteuse* has enough magnetism to start charging fees.

39.

Get all Anal

✳

Or perhaps rectal. The French love suppositories.

In Britain the idea of putting medicine up your bottom is ridiculous. Medicine needs to be swallowed. Unless you can taste how nasty it is, it's unlikely to do you any good. The bottom is where things come out, not where they go in.

However, the rectum is rich in blood vessels that can absorb drugs. A painkiller up the bum may work more quickly on the entire system than one delivered via the stomach. The French particularly value the bottom-up approach for such counter-intuitive complaints as throat conditions. And that's not just talking out of your arse.

Perhaps Anglo-Saxon readers will be unlikely converts. However, consider this simple situation: have you ever tried to administer an oral paracetamol mixture to a screaming baby with a high temperature? Have you watched the baby choke on the medicine, vomit it up, and then have you forced more of it into them, hoping you've got the dosage right, and spent the next few hours worrying that you've killed them? French mothers have none of these worries. During a nappy change, they administer a quick suppository and the baby's temperature comes down within minutes.

Why are French children so well behaved? Almost certainly it's because they know that if they start acting up, their mothers will whip down their *culottes* and administer a sedative.

40.

Be Very Depressed

The French are *the* most depressed nation in the world, according to a 2011 survey by the World Health Organization. Around 89,000 people from all around the world were interviewed, from both high-income and low-income countries. France topped the poll, with 21% of French people reporting a depressive episode that had had a serious impact on their lives. The USA came next at 19.2%, with the world average around 15%. Developed countries in general came off worse. People in low-income counties were reportedly much happier, or perhaps more focussed on things like finding food.

Naturally, for a nation prone to moody self-examination, the results of the survey were endlessly picked over. What could be the reason? The economy? The fact that Christmas comes earlier every year? The exaggerated respect given to philosophers? Too many people with clipboards asking questions?

The finding was not duplicated among Québécois, which seems to indicate that living in continental Europe is a factor. Maybe there is a surprising conclusion to be drawn from all of this. If the French want to be mentally healthier, they should stop rejecting American culture, and in fact entirely surround themselves with Americans and Canadians.

41.

Heal Your Ills at Lourdes

Lourdes has a history of religious controversy. During the 8th century it was occupied by one Mirat, a Saracen prince, who refused to surrender to Charlemagne, king of the Franks. During the siege that followed, an eagle flew over Mirat's stronghold and dropped a colossal trout at his feet. As can be imagined, this completely demoralized him. He saw that the game was up, and converted to Christianity.

Of course, Lourdes is best known for its Marian shrine. Bernadette Soubirous (1844-79), a 14-year-old peasant girl, was out collecting firewood with her two sisters one day in February 1858 when she saw a vision. She afterwards identified the vision as *aquero*, or 'that'. Asked for a more detailed description, she said that it was *uo petito damizelo* ('a small young lady' in Gascon Occitan) of about twelve years of age, i.e. two years younger than herself. She also said that the *damizelo* was smaller than herself, and since Bernadette was very small (about 4 feet 4 inches) this may sound more like an elf or fairy than the Virgin Mary. Some have placed Bernadette's visions in the context of a culture that associated healing springs with sprites and fairy-folk.

Nevertheless Lourdes became a site of worldwide pilgrimage and is currently visited by about 5 million people per year, all coming to drink the water and hoping for a cure for what ails them.

Bernadette, who was canonized in 1933, is at the heart of the whole business, and her indomitable, slightly cussed personality is compelling even to non-believers. On first seeing the vision and reporting it to her parents, she was beaten. She persisted in her claims even when local townsfolk threatened to send her to an asylum. And when, a few years later, a statue was erected to represent the *damizelo*, she declared herself profoundly disappointed by it.

42.

Have a Glass of Chartreuse

Type of drink: liqueur
Colour: dirty green or dirty yellow
Alcohol content: 55% for green, 40% for yellow
Date introduced: 1764 for green, 1838 for yellow
Sole manufacturers: two elderly Carthusian monks in Voiron, near Grenoble

It's true: all the Chartreuse in the world is made by just these two monks, Dom Benoît and Brother Jean-Jacques. These gentlemen, the only ones with the secret recipe, must pass on their knowledge to those who will succeed them. It may be a long time before that happens, though, because Chartreuse is not just a liqueur, it's a miracle health food.

Chartreuse was originally created as an 'Elixir of Life', after a manuscript detailing its preparation was gifted to the Carthusian monks of the monastery of Vauvert, Paris, in 1605. It took the monks many years to decode the manuscript and prepare the Elixir, during which time many had died due to its lack. But immortality was just around the corner. Green Chartreuse, which took its colour from a mixture of 130 different herbs, was created in 1764. After the Revolution of 1789, the monks were expelled by anticlerical Deists, and went to live in Spain. In 1858 they were allowed back under Napoleon, and created Yellow Chartreuse to celebrate, but then were dealt a further blow in 1905 when the laically-minded State (*L'État, c'est moi; votre Chartreuse, c'est à moi*) appropriated all church property.

It's not known how much Chartreuse you have to drink to attain immortality, but a few glasses is more than enough to attain immorality.

French Activities

43.

Re-make the World

This typical French activity – *refaire le monde* – is usually performed over a few drinks, possibly also a few cheeses. Its loose British equivalent is 'setting the world to rights', though in Britain this will be attempted by two blokes in a dreary boozer and is doomed to laughable failure. In France, when *on refait le monde*, one makes a serious attempt to get to the bottom of things with a group of like-minded friends, perhaps at a dinner party, café, picnic or other informal gathering. One argues passionately for one's point of view, and at the end of it all, one feels one has plumbed the depths, shared something of oneself, looked a few eternal verities squarely in the eye, and, in short, really achieved something.

Topics for re-making the world: Why do we need politicians? What is love? What is France? What is morality? What is the difference between high and low culture? What are the responsibilities of the state, and what should be its limits? Is war the engine of history? Do French people avoid uncertainty? Are French men feminine? Are French women masculine? Do British women get old and fat? And so on.

This may sound a familiar sort of activity, even to Anglo-Saxon readers, but just stop for a minute and imagine a group of English twenty-somethings doing this over the course of several hours on a drowsy summer's day – enthusiastically sharing ideas, opinions, and theories – without getting pissed to the point of unconsciousness, shouting, taking their clothes off or terrorizing the community. It's not something we actually do. And yet in France it's a sort of institution.

In summary, the French believe that it's worth setting some serious time aside to look at the big questions.

44.

Negotiate Labyrinths of Bureaucracy

❁

Only eminent Frenchmen are allowed in the Panthéon (see §56). However, if they ever decide to admit foreigners, the first should be Franz Kafka.

Or else perhaps there should be a statue to him outside the *École Nationale d'Administration* in Strasbourg.

No one knows the precise number of France's civil servants, or *fonctionnaires*, but estimates have been put at as high as 20% of the entire population, all devoted to issuing permits, overseeing form-filling, and telling people to go to Window Number 17. In English we would call them, derisively, 'pen-pushers': the French are rather more bitter, calling them *chieurs d'encre* ('ink-shitters').

For example, a certain department in charge of issuing a permit to import antiques tells you that you can be issued with said permit if you turn up during business hours at the appropriate office 50 kilometres from your home. You do so, and when you get there are told that you should have phoned beforehand to let them know you were coming. Or a cash machine has malfunctioned and sucked your euros back into the wall: you go into the bank to complain, and are told to write a letter to the appropriate official, informing them of the situation. Who is the appropriate official? 'I am,' comes the reply. But I've just told you...

One characteristic of French bureaucracy is that everyone reserves the right to disagree with their colleagues. If one official says it's Staircase K, third corridor on the right, another official will swear it's Staircase L. 'They've sent you to the wrong place.' 'You have been misinformed.' 'Please take your dossier with its doorstop of forms and translations and apply to Window 3B, Corridor 15, Staircase F instead. Only not now, because they're closing in ten minutes and the next three days are holidays.'

45.

Spot a *Catherinette*

❋

A *Catherinette* is the name given to any young woman who is unmarried by the age of twenty-five on St Catherine's Day, November 25th. *Catherinettes*, in the absence of husbands, amuse themselves by making headdresses for statues of St Catherine in churches, and also hats for themselves to be worn at St Catherine's Day balls. These hats can be very elaborate, and signify to any passing male that the *Catherinette* in question is available. This is one of those French customs that is so full of good sense that it should be adopted by the rest of the world *tout de suite*, and perhaps extended to other days of the year.

It may be said of any unmarried young woman that *elle va coiffer Sainte Catherine* ('She is making a hat for St Catherine'.)

Of course, social attitudes about women and marriage have changed. Not so many young women enjoy decorating church statues, and twenty-five is no age at all. But St Catherine's Day balls still exist, and young women still need to find partners. So they gamely continue to make hats.

St Catherine herself, meanwhile, has had a rocky road. She was the 17-year-old saint who died in the persecutions of the emperor Maxentius in the 4th century: after refusing to convert, the emperor sent 50 pagan philosophers to debate with her, and she converted them all to Christianity. The emperor had the philosophers petulantly killed, and sentenced Catherine to be broken on a spiked wheel. Unfortunately the Catholic Church decided in 1969 that Catherine probably didn't, after all, exist; and in 2002 her feast day became an 'optional memorial'.

46.

Drive a 2CV

❋

The 2CV holds the same place in the French imagination as the Mini does in the British or the Beetle does in the German. Small but indomitable, ugly but tenacious, unpretentious yet iconic, it the ultimate rebuff to autophobes who claim that cars can't have personalities: its bulbous-eye headlamps make it seem almost alive, and its gawkiness and unapologetic clunkiness make it the epitome of a certain type of French post-war utilitarian knowhow. Its design has given rise to numerous nicknames: the Umbrella on Four Wheels, the Upside-down Perambulator, the Duck, the Goat, the Flying Dustbin and the Tin Snail. All are more or less affectionate.

Citroën began production of the 2CV in 1948: its name means *Deux chevaux*, or 'two horses', which gives you an idea of the size of its engine. Its lack of speed and acceleration has led some to claim that in order to merge onto a motorway you need to make a written application first. It was originally designed for farmers and other lower-income persons buying their first car, and the brief was that it should carry four people, consume very little fuel, perform well on country roads or indeed off-road, and 'carry a basket of eggs without breaking any'. Later, in the 1960s, it became popular with students and hippies, since it was cheap and easy to repair.

Of course, most people in France these days would prefer to drive a BMW. But get behind the wheel of a 2CV and observe French people's reactions as you pass by: you will see in their faces not so much national pride as bittersweet nostalgia for a bygone era when life was simpler, the goose-livers fatter, the air cleaner, and everyone was younger, happier, and had longer hair.

47.

Ride the TGV
(when it isn't on strike)

❁

The *Train à Grande Vitesse* (High Speed Train) is one of the glories of France. Opened in 1981 to connect Paris and Lyon, it now plies several routes connecting French cities and even surrounding countries (including the UK: the Eurostar is essentially a TGV modified for the narrower British track gauge). It is the fastest wheeled train in the world, achieving in 2007 the astonishing speed of 357.2 mph, although its regular point-to-point average speed is closer to 200 mph (still, of course, very quick). In fact, for many journeys, the TGV is faster than an aeroplane. The ride itself is very smooth, noiseless (from the inside) and comfortable.

There's another even more impressive thing about the TGV – the price. Although tickets are not exactly cheap, the TGV was intended from the first to be comparable to existing conventional lines, and not a method of travel for a wealthy elite. The TGV slogan, 'Progress means nothing unless it is shared by all', went right to the heart of French egalitarianism. As a result, TGVs have now clocked up around 1.5 billion passenger journeys.

Naturally the TGV is not immune to the French love of a labour dispute, so trains are only very fast, efficient, democratic etc. where available. But one can't hold that against them. The TGV wouldn't be very French without grinding to a halt occasionally.

In a rather nice French touch, bridges on lines used by the TGV have sensors to detect objects that people have thrown onto the tracks. This is to stop disgruntled farmers committing mass murder.

48.

Dress Up for *Carnaval* and Pay your Respects on *Toussaint*

❀

Carnival season is between Christmas and Lent in the Christian calendar, though the biggest French carnival celebration is Mardi Gras, or 'Fat Tuesday', the day before the beginning of Lent. The original idea seems to have been to use up the last remaining scraps of food before the Lenten season, but human ingenuity and love of a good time have taken over. Typical French carnivalling behaviour involves outlandish and magnificent costumes, masking, parades, sporting competitions, dancing, feasting and licentiousness of all types and varieties: one tradition is the 'burning of Monsieur Carnaval', in which an effigy is torched to atone for the sins of the French during the previous year, while revellers dance around singing:

Adieu pauvre Carnaval. Tu t'en vas et moi je reste pour manger la soupe à l'ail. ('Goodbye Mister

Carnival. You're going and I'm staying here eating garlic soup.')

At the other end of the year, the commemoration of the dead takes place on All Saints Day, November 1st, known in France as *Toussaint*. This is a public holiday (though in French law, if the holiday falls at the weekend, that's hard luck, and people do their best to *faire le pont* in the most outrageous manner – see §28 – to make up for it). The following day, November 2, or All Souls Day (*Commémoration des fidèles défunts*), is when dead relatives are supposed to be commemorated, but the French, ever-practical, commemorate them on the day when they are off work. Families spend time together visiting the graves of family members or loved ones, placing chrysanthemums on the grave and lighting candles in church. *Toussaint* is the antithesis to Mardi Gras: restrained, respectful, and an occasion for people to spend time together and cement family bonds.

49.

Support the Bastards

These are *Les Enfoirés* – meaning 'the bastards' or 'the tossers'. *Les Enfoirés* are an association of musicians put together by the comic actor Coluche in 1986 for the purpose of charity fundraising, and they're very close to the French heart. To give an idea in Anglo-Saxon terms, one might think of a rolling Live Aid that never goes away.

Les Enfoirés began in 1985 when Coluche started *Les Restos du Coeur*, or 'The Restaurants of the Heart'. The idea behind *Les Restos* was to supply meals to people on the breadline through a national chain of soup kitchens in public places. Being French, of course, there was a choice of bisque or consommé and croutons were included either way. Coluche then instituted *Les Enfoirés*, a group of musician friends, to raise money for *Les Restos*. After his death in 1986, the concerts were continued in his memory, and even now, nearly thirty years after his death, Coluche is the fifth most-loved man in France.

Les Enfoirés do a great deal more than supply meals (though they do a lot of that – there are almost 2,500 *Restos*, staffed by 66,000 volunteers, which supply around 130 million meals per year). They organize cultural events, hold picnics, supply clothing and shelter, and in fact do everything that any large domestic charity would do. So any homeless person can say with justification: 'I owe it all to the bastards.'

50.

Get in Touch with your Inner Child

If you want to see the French at their most alarming, go to a Chantal Goya concert. Chantal Goya is a French chanteuse familiar to every citizen over 35. Her main hits include 'Bécassine, c'est ma cousine', about a Breton girl (Bécassine) in a famous newspaper cartoon – which led the Breton singer Dan Ar Braz to release a song called 'Bécassine, ce n'est pas ma cousine' – and 'Ce matin, un lapin', about a rabbit who kills a hunter. People who attend her shows regress to childhood, wearing rabbit costumes, pretending to be rabbits, and giving themselves over entirely to nostalgia and whimsy – even grown men with carefully styled facial hair who probably spend their days trying to chat up American women on the métro.

It's strange how a body of water twenty miles wide can do this. Witness the Casimir phenomenon. Casimir is an orange dinosaur who must have been the prototype for the eminently dynamitable Barney. Casimir is funny, huggable and kind, and his favourite food is 'Gloubi-Boulga', the recipe of which comprises a mixture of strawberry jam, grated chocolate, banana, very strong mustard and Toulouse sausages (warm but not cooked). When the popularity of Casimir was at its height, thousands of French adults were in the habit of turning up at his 'Gloubi-Boulga nights', which involved dressing up as characters from children's TV of the 80s, and pretending to enjoy sweets, soft drinks and balloons.

The French, like the Japanese, also enjoy the inexcusable vacuum that is Mickey Mouse. That is really all that needs to be said.

51.

Play the Goatee Game

◉

This is a children's game. It has no English equivalent, though something like 'slapsies' would be close. To play, you hold each other's chin lightly with your hand, look into one another's eyes, and recite the rhyme:

> *Je te tiens, tu me tiens, par la barbichette;*
> *Le premier de nous deux qui rira, aura une tapette!*

> I hold you, you hold me, by the chinny-chin;
> The first of us to laugh, will have a little slap!

As the rhyme suggests, the object is to punish the one who cracks first: if no one cracks, a light tickling of the chin is sometimes practised. The first to smile or laugh receives a slap, and the game re-commences.

Barbichette literally means 'little beard' or 'goatee'. The word *tapette* is more problematic: it has a secondary meaning of 'homosexual'. For this reason *giflette* ('little slap') is sometimes substituted.

When trying your hand at the game, the rhyme needs to be pronounced by sounding the silent 'e', or *e muet*, at the end of the word *barbichette*. This phenomenon is most familiar to English-speakers from another rhyme, 'Frère Jacques', where the final 'e' of 'Frère' and the 'es' of 'Jacques' are treated as separate syllables. Thus the pronunciation of the rhyme is:

> *Je te tiens, tu me tiens, par la barbichet-te;*
> *Le premier de nous deux qui rira, aura une tapette!*

52.

Go to a *Vide-Grenier*

A *vide-grenier* is the French equivalent of a car-boot sale. It literally means 'empty attic', and was no doubt proposed by the *Académie française* to stop people referring to *un car-boot*.

A slight difference to a traditional UK car-boot sale is that in a *vide-grenier* the cars are often lined up on the side of the road, so that you process down an avenue of junk, rather than wandering around a playing-field of junk. However, *vide-greniers* are held in parks, town squares and playing-fields too.

Vide-greniers often eschew the trestle table and go for the 'bomb aftermath' look, with wares just spread haphazardly on the ground.

At a *vide-grenier* you will find the following items: a selection of enormous keys that look like they could unlock the doors in a novel by Alexandre Dumas *fils*; a horribly soiled Dell D430; an enamel sign saying *Cabine téléphonique*; a sewing pattern for a dress from the 1940s; a standing chin-high bird-cage; a Smurf figurine with the paint sucked off.

Vide-greniers are supposedly for amateurs, not professionals, and exhibitors are restricted to two *vides* a year. What this boils down to is that you need to apply for a licence well in advance, submit your photo ID, and pay a fee by going to Window Number 3b, Corridor F (see §44).

A *vide-grenier* is not the same as a *brocante*. A *brocante* follows the same sort of format, i.e. it is held outside by people wearing gloves, except that it is openly professionalized and features real antique dealers, booksellers, etc. This is the theory, at any rate. Those who have come across stalls at *vide-greniers* selling only new training shoes may reserve the right to be sceptical.

French Places

53.

Visit the Sculpted Rocks
of Abbé Fouré

❁

The term *art brut*, or, as English-speaking readers
might know it, 'outsider art', is a French invention:
it was coined in the early twentieth century by the
artist Jean Dubuffet to describe works of art created
outside the usual art establishment, e.g. by the insane, the imprisoned or children. The works of Abbé
Fouré are generally considered an example of *art
brut* to rank alongside examples such as the Palace
of Facteur Cheval (see the next section) or the Watts
Towers of Los Angeles.

Abbé Fouré was Adolphe-Julien Fouré, born in
1863, who served as a priest in Brittany before being
dismissed from his post following a dispute with
his superiors. In 1894 he retired to a wooden shack
at Rothéneuf on the Brittany coast, not far from
Saint-Malo, and began a new career as an artist.

What the Abbé did was to sculpt the rocks

around his home to feature various religious and folkloric figures. We have the Blessed Virgin with the nations of the world prostrating themselves at her feet; we have a local family of legend who plied a trade as pirates; we have grotesque heads, phallic watchers of the sea, and sprawling, crawling figures, inspired by and originating in the shapes of the rocks themselves. The Abbé also completed hundreds of wooden sculptures, and had postcards printed featuring himself posing with his work: these he sold to raise money for the poor.

The Abbé's cabin no longer exists, but his stone sculptures can still be seen in all their obsessive magnificence.

54.

Visit the Ideal Temple
of the Facteur Cheval

Facteur Cheval, or 'the Postman Cheval', was Ferdinand Cheval (1836-1924), who spent the last thirty-three years of his life building what he termed a *Palais idéal* near the town of Hauterives in southeast France.

Like the sculpted rocks of Abbé Fouré, the *Palais idéal* was a personal project with an *art brut* flavour, conceived and completed by M Cheval himself. And like the sculpted rocks, it is now a national monument, open to the public.

The palace is not easy to describe. One might say it looks like a realisation of the paintings of Max Ernst mixed with the teeming figures of a Hindu temple, except that Facteur Cheval's work preceded that of Max Ernst by a couple of decades, and Ernst and the Surrealists were in fact inspired by M Cheval, not the other way around. The palace is made of pebbles embedded in lime cement, and is not petty in scale: it features towers, battlements, grottoes, temples, statues and stairways, and because of its pebble-based construction looks like a sandcastle made by a child with an infinity of time and no sea to wash it away.

Of the genesis of his project, M Cheval had this to say:

> My foot tripped on a stone that almost made me fall. I wanted to know what it was... It was a stone of such a strange shape that I put it in my pocket to admire it at my ease. The next day, I went back to the same place. I found more stones, even more beautiful, I gathered them together on the spot and was overcome with delight... I said to myself: since Nature is willing to do the sculpture, I will do the masonry and the architecture.

55.

Enter the Abode of Chaos

A third specimen in this trilogy of French outsider art is the Abode of Chaos (*Demeure de Chaos*). This is a former 17th-century coaching inn at Saint-Romain-au-Mont-d'Or near Lyon, which has been transformed into a museum – or, if you agree with its critics, a junkyard – by its owner, Thierry Ehrmann. Ehrmann happens to be the wealthy CEO of a prominent French company, which is helpful, since he can afford to contest the various lawsuits that are currently being waged against him to restore the coaching inn to its former state.

The theme of the Abode of Chaos is the post-apocalyptic nature of pre-apocalyptic modern life. The inn and its grounds are essentially a polychrome war-zone, featuring giant skulls in trees, a downed helicopter, huge portraits of Nelson Mandela and Osama bin Laden and various other artworks in an *art brut*, *art trouvé* and *art apocalyptique* style.

Admission is free, and visitors can take home a free book and poster prominently featuring the words 'Shame on You'.

The museum taps into some interesting currents in French life. What should take precedence, the art of the modern day, or the vernacular architecture of the 17th century? What is the difference between a national treasure and an eyesore (one recalls that the Eiffel Tower itself was originally reviled)? What is the relation between France's urban communities, with their ethnic and class diversity, and the sleepy rural life of a place like Saint-Romain-au-Mont-d'Or? Does France truly cherish its outsider artists – such as the Abbé Fouré, the Facteur Cheval, and M Ehrmann – or do they exist in spite of France?

M Ehrmann's fight has now been taken to European Court of Human Rights, and at the time of going to press the situation does not look good: you may wish to make your visit sooner rather than later.

56.

Visit the Panthéon

The Panthéon is an ex-church in Paris's Latin Quarter. In appearance it looks rather like St Paul's, with a neoclassical colonnaded exterior and dome. These days it serves as a secular burial-place for the great men of France. They include Voltaire, Jean-Jacques Rousseau, Victor Hugo, Émile Zola, Alexandre Dumas *père*, Louis Braille, Joseph Louis Lagrange, André Malraux, Toussaint Louverture, Jean Jaurès and 61 others.

Above the entrance to the Panthéon is the gigantic capitalized inscription *AUX GRANDS HOMMES LA PATRIE RECONNAISSANTE* ('To great men, from their grateful nation'). It is often said that Marie Curie is the only woman buried in the Panthéon, though in fact there are two: the other is Sophie Berthelot, wife of the chemist Marcellin Berthelot, who was buried there to keep her husband company. This has caused much controversy in recent years, with activists calling for a 'Pink Panthéon' including women such as Simone de Beauvoir, Jeanne d'Arc, Coco Chanel, Colette, Germaine de Staël, Marguerite Duras, Anaïs Nin, Edith Piaf, George Sand and Marie Antoinette. In 2014 Francois Hollande bowed to the pressure and announced that two more women were to be admitted: the wartime Resistance heroines Germaine Tillion and Geneviève de Gaulle-Anthonioz.

Nothing, however, has yet been done about the inscription, which mentions only *HOMMES*.

57

Descend into the Catacombs

Paris has three undergrounds: 1) the métro; 2) the metaphorical radical underground; and 3) the catacombs, which are non-metaphorical but actually more metaphorical than the real metaphorical underground. This is because no one really knows their extent, and, more than that, they are full of untellable stories of the dead. They are a place of the imagination, the Id of Paris.

The catacombs comprise two related systems. The first are old limestone mine workings, situated largely to the south of Paris. These were made by tunnelling beneath the city, following the seams of stone. When these seams were worked out, they were simply abandoned: there are reckoned to be hundreds of kilometres of them. The second system is the ossuaries, largely following the mine-workings, which are extensive enough to house the mortal remains of six million dead Parisians. When you visit, descending via a stone staircase at the former Barrière d'Enfer city gate, and walk for about a mile, you will find yourself standing before a portal, the entry to the colossal boneyard, with the inscription *Arrête! C'est ici l'empire de la Mort* ('Stop! Here is the Empire of Death'). Beyond are more bones than a thousand Idéfixes could dream of, stacked in walls of tibia, fibia, femora and skulls, arranged in patterns of hearts, circles and crucifixes.

In their function as an Empire of Death and the Imagination, the catacombs are the playground of Paris's artists, activists, spelunkers and cataphiles. They have also played their part in many of Paris's historical moments. Communards, French Resistance fighters and Nazi soldiers all hunkered down here and left their graffiti.

It is often thought that the reason there are not many tall buildings in Paris is because French architects are tasteful and restrained. In fact, in some areas, the *souterrain* is so riddled with holes that any heavy structures would collapse.

58.

Go to the World's Oldest Art Gallery

This is to be found in the caves of Lascaux, situated near the village of Montignac in the Dordogne. The caves contain art from the Late Stone Age (from about 50,000 years to about 10,000 years ago). Experts disagree on the precise date of the paintings, but guesses tend to cluster around 20,000 BC. They depict mainly large animals: horses, stags, cattle, bison and big cats, plus various dotted designs and geometric shapes. Some of the paintings are very large, the largest a bull about five metres long. Altogether there are about 2,000 animals, in black, yellow and red pigments, often layered over one another, as if composition was not as important as the act of painting itself. The various rooms in the cave-complex include the Hall of the Bulls, the Chamber of Felines, the Shaft and the Nave.

The caves were discovered by an 18-year-old apprentice garage mechanic, Marcel Ravidat, in 1940, some say while looking for his dog Robot. They were opened to the public in 1948, and were soon receiving more than a thousand visitors a day; but conservators began to notice that the paintings were deteriorating. It was realised that the carbon dioxide exhaled by the multitude was stripping away the pigments. The caves were closed for restorations, and a replica cave opened nearby in 1963; this replica cave is the cave that is now open for visitors. Meanwhile the real cave continues to suffer from problems. Various epidemics of mould have invaded its surfaces, possibly caused by strong lights, the air conditioning system, or the continuing exhalations of conservators. Even the replica cave is having trouble.

The Lascaux paintings have had an important influence on modern art. Picasso is said to have seen them and commented 'We have learned nothing.' One modern comparison might be to the drawings of Ronald Searle (who lived most of his life in France). Some of the Lascaux cows' faces have a Searlish quality.

59.

Visit Carnac

Carnac in Brittany is Europe's most extensive prehistoric site. Three locations – Ménec, Kermario and Kerlescan – contain more than 3,000 standing stones, arranged in lines stretching hundreds of metres, all of local granite and dating to the Neolithic period, probably from 4,000 to 3,000 BC. Near the lines of stones are a selection of other megalithic objects: dolmens (usually consisting of a large flat stone balanced on one or more standing stones, possibly tomb-markers), stone circles (now mostly vanished) and miscellaneous monoliths such as the Manio Giant (which is over 6 metres tall). There are also various tumuli, i.e. mounds of earth housing the bodies and grave-goods of the wealthier prehistoric folk.

It's no longer allowed to wander freely among the stones, but there are official guided tours that can be booked in advance. There's also a Museum of Prehistory, in which many of the objects that were plundered from the tumuli are on show; and the Maison des Mégalithes, which gives information on the history of the site.

What was the purpose of the stones at Carnac? Its builders left no handbook. The earliest common interpretation was that they were the site of the Druidic cult (an interpretation we also find in *Asterix and the Golden Sickle*), but others have claimed they were an aid to astronomical observation, or even a means of detecting earthquakes.

Local beliefs attribute them to the remnants of a Roman legion turned to stone by Merlin. Breton resistance has very ancient roots. *Nous sommes en 50 avant Jésus-Christ; toute la Gaule est occupée par les Romains... Toute? Non! Car un village peuplé d'irréductibles Gaulois résiste encore et toujours à l'envahisseur...*

60

Go to a Roman Amphitheatre

Gaul, after being defeated 1-0 at Alesia in 52BC, was forced to submit to the Roman yoke. But there were some compensations. Gladiatorial shows, chariot-races, executions, wild-beast hunts, mock-naval combats, the very *crème de la crème* of drama and poetry: the best and worst of the entire ancient world was suddenly available to subscribers at very reasonable rates. In fact performances were usually free, to distract the conquered from political activity.

France, unlike Britain, has an amazing number of these surviving Roman entertainment centres. They include the Theatre of Orange in the Rhône valley, with its magnificent and unique stone backdrop, one of the best-preserved Roman theatres in the world and a UNESCO World Heritage site, still used for theatrical performances and the venue for the summer opera festival, the *Chorégies d'Orange*. Then there is the theatre complex at Lyon, dating to the late first century BC, where there are ruins of three ancient Roman structures – a theatre, odeum and temple – on Fourvière Hill. Also not to be missed is the Arles amphitheatre, one of the places in southern France where one can still see bullfighting (Van Gogh, who lived there, painted it), an arena so big that in the medieval period 200 homes were built inside it.

61.

See the Lyon Festival of Lights

This is a four day festival around December 8th every year, and celebrates Lyon's deliverance from the plague in the seventeenth century. And indeed, if you go to Lyon, very few people have the plague there even today.

Ordinary families place candles in stained-glass holders on their windowsills, which makes the entire city very pretty, but the 'Festival of Lights' is really to do with the grand municipal projects that illuminate the city's prominent buildings and landmarks, particularly the Basilica of Fourvière and the statue of the Virgin next to it. These spectacular shows, created by France's greatest contemporary artists, draw crowds of millions every year from all around the world, making it one of the largest of all international festivals.

The shows are not merely the projection of coloured light: many are inspired by fine art, photography and cinema, even literature. One building might be transformed into a canvas by Seurat; another might be wrapped in scenes from *Le Petit prince* (Lyon was Saint-Exupéry's home town); another might feature an enormous eye, as if from Buñuel's film *L'Age d'or*. Overhead, a series of weird geometric shapes, visitors from another galaxy, float over the heads of the spectators.

One of the beauties of the Lyon festival is that it retains a spiritual quality; it is not, as with the Oktoberfest or the Rio Carnival, just a gigantic excuse for a booze-up. It has its meditative aspects. Along with the light shows and events are also special religious services, international masses, nativity scenes and torch-lit processions.

62.

Visit the *Dune du Pilat*

❀

Some Frequently Asked Questions:

Q. What is the Dune du Pilat?
A. It is Europe's tallest sand dune, at around 110 metres. It is 500 metres wide, 2.7 km long and 60,000,000 cubic metres in volume. The Dune is located in the Arcachon Bay, 60 km south of Bordeaux, and is currently moving inland at the rate of 3 metres per year, swallowing up trees, houses, roads and small animals. It is known by locals as 'The Monster'.

Q. When can I visit the Dune?
A. Whenever you like. There are no opening hours. It's a sand dune.

Q. Is there any car park near the Dune?
A. You bet there is. There are around a million

visitors a year to the Dune, coming by car, coach, bicycle, solar-powered bus, etc., to enjoy climbing the Dune.

Q. Am I allowed to take my dog to the Dune?
A. If you don't, the Dune may come to your dog.

Q. What is the best season to visit the Dune?
A. Whenever you want to see sand.

Q. Is there any restaurant near the Dune?
A. Of course there is. You're in France.

Q. What specialities can be enjoyed near the Dune?
A. You can enjoy oysters from Arcachon Bay, local dishes including duck confit with mush-rooms, etc., as well as all the wines of the Aquit-aine region, specially strained to remove the sand.

Q. Do they serve ortolan at the Dune?
A. Definitely not. Ortolan is illegal.

63.

Recharge your Batteries at the World's Largest Solar Furnace

❁

It's difficult to give an idea of the bizarre magnificence of the solar furnace at Odeillo in the French Pyrenees. It looks rather like the Arc de Triomphe has been cut into pieces, silvered all over and rearranged by Jean Tinguely.

Built in 1969 from earlier prototypes by an obsessive French solar scientist (Felix Thrombe), it is the largest machine of its type in the world, consisting of a field of 10,000 mirrors arranged on the side of a hill. These bounce sunlight onto an enormous parabolic solar mirror covering almost 2,000 square metres. This light is then re-concentrated onto an area the size of a Druidic cauldron, which is thereby heated to temperatures around two-thirds of the surface temperature of the sun (in excess of 3,200 degrees Celsius). The resulting energy can be used to generate power, melt steel, or make hydrogen fuel.

Because the solar furnace is located in the Pyrenees, in a climate that enjoys 300 sunny days per year, and where the air is exceptionally clean and fresh, and because the parabolic mirror reflects the entire surrounding countryside in an extraordinary way, and because, in fact, the solar furnace at Odeillo shows us the only sane and reasonable path for the energy future of our species, it's rather a nice place for a day out.

64.

Hike Up an Active Volcano

La Réunion is an island in the Indian Ocean. Find
Madagascar on a map, turn right and you're there. It
was first occupied by France in the 1640s and admin-
istered as a colony for three centuries, its population,
largely of slaves, labouring to produce sugar cane: in
1946 it was made a *département* of France. *La Réunion* is thus as much France as Paris is. It joins the
other *départements et territoires d'outre-mer* ('overseas
departments and territories'), referred to with Gallic
brevity as the DOM-TOMs: Guadeloupe, Marti-
nique, French Guiana and Mayotte. (There are also
the COMs, or *collectivités d'outre-mer*, such as French
Polynesia, making the entire possessions the DOM-
TOM-COMs.)

La Réunion is one of the few places in France you
can hike up an active volcano. The *Piton de la Four-
naise* ('Peak of the Furnace'), is located on the east-
ern side of the island, and is one of the most active

volcanos in the world: eruptions occurred in 2006, 2007, 2008 and 2010, and more are expected. In vulcanological language, its eruption style is termed 'effusive'. The eruptions typically produce lava rather than the more devastating pyroclastic flows, but the lava field can be extensive, reaching the ocean: little habitation or infrastructure is thus possible to the east of the caldera. Visitors may however climb the volcano during its dormant periods.

Geologically, the area of land between the caldera and the ocean is weak, and a major seismic event could prompt a catastrophic collapse into the ocean, triggering a megatsunami that would radiate across the ocean, drowning Mauritius to the east, and affecting Australia, Indonesia, India and as far north as the coast of Oman.

France is safe, however.

65

Journey to the Centre of the Earth

On 19 September 1963, Salvador Dali was sitting in the train station at Perpignan in the extreme south of France. Suddenly he had an epiphany. Perpignan station was at the centre of the world. Just as Jerusalem had formerly featured as the earth's navel, now Perpignan train station should be considered the focus of all of mankind's hopes, dreams and fantasies.

The newsreel footage of Dali announcing his discovery can still be viewed – particularly if you are in Perpignan, where they have a copy of it. 'The station of Perpignan is destined to become one of the most important cosmic places in the Dalinian cosmogony,' Dali enunciates, his eyes bulging rapaciously. 'Every time I see the station of Perpignan I discover in my brain such utterly sublime ideas that it is a kind of veritable mental ejaculation, that my friends practically have to prop me up because I become exhausted. And I have arrived at the conclusion that all the great inventions of humanity, all of them, took place at the exact centre of the station of Perpignan.'

In 1965, Dali unveiled a painting that demonstrated the truth of this proposition. *La Gare de Perpignan* ('Perpignan Train Station') shows four beams of orange light converging on an indistinct head of Christ wearing the crown of thorns. Flanking Christ on the right and left are figures from the Millet's painting 'The Angelus' (an obsession of Dali from childhood), which shows two peasants praying in a field. Also on the right, two figures appear to be copulating. A locomotive careens onto the canvas at the top. Two figures of Dali jump, spreadeagled.

The 'greatest inventions of humanity' thus prove to be sex, prayer, trains and Dali himself, which is perhaps not so inaccurate.

French Crimes

66.

Jaywalk

※

This is very much a French thing to do, but there is a conundrum: there is no word for 'jaywalk' in French, so there is no sense that a French person could actually do it. This poses all sorts of philosophical problems. Is language prior to experience? Is what is legal what is moral? Does existence precede essence, or is it the other way around?

The actual legal situation is in flux. Formerly, pedestrians could be fined four euros for crossing a highway if there was a pedestrian crossing closer than 50 metres. The fiddly measurements involved, and the paltry amount of the fine itself, meant that it was hardly ever enforced. In fact, the French Highway Code currently requires drivers to give way to pedestrians, though not many French drivers are ever seen to be doing so.

Perhaps it's that familiar beast, French individualism, that is at the root of it. In Japan, no one crosses against the light, or crosses a road at any other point than a designated pedestrian crossing; but Japan is a highly collective culture in which virtue is social. France is a culture in which virtue is individual. Governments and leaders are accepted as a necessary evil, and true loyalties are to smaller entities: the family and the self. *I* want to cross the road *now*, and your petty rules – however good they might be for other people and the harmonious running of society in general – aren't going to stop *me*; *I* am more important than a half-ton lump of speeding metal, though I am also softer and squelchier.

The fact that one of France's greatest 20th-century philosophers, Roland Barthes, was run down by a bread van, is probably no coincidence.

67.

Visit *L'Auberge Rouge*

❀

This is the Red Inn, situated in the commune of La-narce in Ardèche. In the early nineteenth century it was the site of a series of cannibalistic murders that have somewhat taken hold of the French imagination.

What seems to have happened is that the inn-keeper and his wife, Pierre and Marie Martin, along with their domestic help and factotum Jean Rochette (known as 'Fetish'), murdered more than fifty travellers, ostensibly for their possessions, but also because they liked it. When their depredations were finally brought to light in 1833, the trio were executed in front of their inn, watched by a mob of 30,000 people, with 'Fetish' screaming: 'Cursed masters, what have you not made me do!'

The horrors uncovered at their trial have been endlessly recounted in ballads, books, films and folklore. While one clutched a sleeping victim, another would pour oil hot or molten lead into their mouth; the corpses would be burned in the oven, releasing a pall of death over the countryside; Mme Martin would serve customers with stews made from body parts of previous guests; and the whole hotel, from the bedsheets to the baguettes, was spattered with blood and lymph, which makes one wonder why the Martins went undetected for so long.

The current building has hardly changed since 1831, and now houses a museum that can be visited by the ghoulish.

68.

Kill Over Truffles

❁

This is precisely what happened in 2010. Laurent Rambaud, a 32-year-old farmer from the southern French region of Drôme, shot and killed a trespasser who he suspected was after his truffles (*truffes* in French). Rambaud was arrested and imprisoned, but his ordeal was lightened by the many hundreds of supporters who clamoured outside the jail for his release. In Drôme there is zero sympathy for anyone who tries to snaffle truffles.

This might seem surprising, until you realize that the native black truffle of southern France is insanely valuable. Specimens can go for as much as 2,000 euros/kg, and very large single specimens can be sold at auction for hundreds of thousands of euros. The rarity of truffles, and the difficulty of their cultivation, mean that they are surrounded by crime in all its forms. Genuine truffles can be 'cut' with counterfeit truffles imported from China, much as cocaine is 'cut' with baby laxative. French thieves use earth-moving equipment to ram-raid restaurants known to have a truffle stash. Truffles are part of the black economy, because no truffle-hunter wants to pay income tax. The peril surrounding truffles is so great that the truffle market held in Richerenches has a special guard of armed *gendarmes*.

What do truffles taste of that makes them so prized? Well they taste of mushrooms. Or perhaps gasoline. Or perhaps meat. Or perhaps strawberries dipped in cocoa. It depends who you are talking to. If you want to get an idea without paying the price, try drizzling some truffle oil (which is expensive, but not cripplingly so) onto some potatoes. Truffle oil usually doesn't contain any truffles, but is rich in the chemical compounds that give truffles their characteristic flavour.

69.

Destroy All Forgeries

❋

In the UK, if you buy a painting and it turns out to be a forgery, that's just hard luck. You hang it on your wall and ruefully tell visitors you got cheated. In France, you do not have this luxury. Courts can order that forgeries be burnt.

French law asserts the moral right of an artist (*droit à la paternité*) to prevent the use of his name on works that he did not create. This extends well past the life of the artist. The artist's children, grandchildren or executors inherit the *droit à la paternité*, and they and their appointed experts are allowed to say whether or not a particular work is genuine. Thus, on their say-so, an undistinguished drawing bought at a *vide-grenier* (a French car-boot sale) could suddenly be worth millions; conversely, a very distinguished drawing bought for millions could be rendered instantaneously worthless, then forcibly burnt while the owner looks on. In 2012, for example, this led to the *auto-da-fé* of a drawing and a painting claimed to be by Joan Miró, but ruled as a fake by the Paris Court of Appeal.

Opponents of the French system argue that the situation is rather like the death penalty. It is very final. If a fake is destroyed that later turns out to be genuine, then an injustice has been perpetrated. In the art world, works previously deemed to have been fakes are regularly re-authenticated – and then de-authenticated again. Authentication is not an exact science, and experts often work on little more than a sense of what feels right.

Opponents will also point out that perhaps the best people to decide authenticity are not the children or grandchildren of an artist. You wouldn't necessarily want your Michelin-starred dinner prepared by the grandchild of a famous chef.

70.

Join *Les UX*

✻

Anyone who has seen *Delicatessen*, the French film directed by directed by Jean-Pierre Jeunet and Marc Caro, will remember the *Troglodistes*, a band of wet-suit-clad *agents provocateurs* who live in the sewers underneath the city. These seem to have been inspired by real life. A real group calling itself *les UX*, short for 'Urban eXperiment'), was founded in 1981 to exploit Paris's network of tunnels, sewers, crypts and hidden places.

Les UX compose an unknown number of individuals split into groups with discrete responsibilities. A faction known as *La Mexicaine de perforation* ('The Mexican Consolidated Drilling Authority') specialise in underground artistic events: their most notorious creation is a secret illegal cinema underneath the Trocadéro (an area of Paris in the 16th arrondissement) complete with bar and kitchen. The Mouse House, an all-female group, specialize in infiltration (possibly in sweet-talking custodians of national monuments so as to gain illicit access). Another team, called Untergunther, secretly restores ancient monuments. The most famous example of this is the 2006 restoration of the Panthéon clock. What Untergunther did was to take control of a secret entryway to the Panthéon and build a high-tech squat under the dome. From this base, they set about restoring the rusted clock, using the services of rogue clock-maker Jean-Baptiste Viot. The project went entirely undetected until the clock started to chime, upon which the authorities were instructed to wind it occasionally. Four members of Untergunther were then apprehended and tried, but the case was thrown out (and described by a state prosecutor as 'stupid'), because under French law there is no penalty for trying to improve something.

How you join is not known; but it might help if you have your own wetsuit and are unfazed by skulls.

71.

Count the Torched Cars
on New Year's Eve

It is now an established tradition for the Interior Minister to hold a press conference to report on the number of cars set alight by arsonists over the holiday period. In 2014 the number immolated on New Year's Eve was 1,067. This, the minister, Manuel Valls, said, was 'a positive result'; it was 10% down on the previous year.

Some people feel that this official release of figures is a mistake. It only stimulates rival pyromaniacs to try harder.

Car-torching has been a very French problem since the late 90s, when a spate of burnings in Strasbourg led that charming city to be known for something other than its Christmas market. Then in 2005, following the deaths of two teenagers in the Parisian suburb of Clichy-sous-Bois, a wave of riots in the poorer districts of Paris, Toulouse, Marseilles and elsewhere made news all over the world; hundreds of cars were being torched every night, and a state of emergency was declared. Paris became known as the City of Light for a rather different reason.

Vehicle-burning is a sport not restricted to New Year's Eve. Bastille Day, July 14, is another popular date in the torching calendar. In fact, year-round statistics show a staggering 40,211 cars torched in 2011, 37,383 cars in 2012 and 34,441 cars in 2013. The trend, as the government hastens to point out, is downward, but the lowest figures still work out at 94 cars deliberately set alight every day.

Why are cars such a target? They are a symbol of comparative wealth for disaffected unemployed youths, often from poor ethnic minority communities. They also make a loud bang and are fun to watch.

72

Shudder at the Horrific Relics
of the *Musée de la Préfecture*

✸

The *Musée de la Préfecture* (Paris Police Museum) is situated within the actual police station of the 5th arrondissement. Here you can see the entire sweep of Paris's criminal history, from the 17th century to the modern day. One may, for example, examine:

- A prison register showing an entry for the assassin of Henry IV, François Ravaillac, who was subjected to the most extreme public tortures before being executed (the tortures are listed in very beautiful copperplate);
- The actual blade of the guillotine used during the Terror at the Place de Grève (weighing around 10 kg);
- Artefacts from the career of Joseph Philippe, a nineteenth-century murderer

of prostitutes. (Quote: 'I am very fond of women, and I accommodate them in my own way. I first strangle them, then I cut their throats')

- The ticket stub that led to the conviction and execution of Henri Landru in 1922: Landru was accused of the murder of some dozen women, who he took by train to his country retreat. His parsimony was his downfall, since he always bought a return ticket for himself, but only ever a single ticket for his victims;
- The automatic pistol used to assassinate President Doumer in 1932 (the only French president to die of gunshot wounds);
- Artefacts from the career of Marcel Petiot, who during the Second World War lured Jews to his apartment with the promise of a secret escape route from Nazi-occupied Paris, but instead injected them with strychnine, took their valuables and dumped the bodies in a lime pit.

The museum is fascinating and free: cheap thrills indeed.

73.

Bomb a *Paillote*

Perhaps this is less a French thing to do than a Corsican thing to do. The island of Corsica, just off the south-west coast, is, of course, a territorial possession of France, albeit one with certain special privileges. One of those privileges is to resist, violently, any idea that Corsica is French.

The period since the 1970s has seen various bombings, assassinations and attacks on French interests on the island. A particular target has been the holiday homes of wealthy Parisians, particularly developments situated on Corsica's unspoiled coastline. Corsicans don't want their beautiful island turned into a replica of the Costa del Sol. And they have other grievances: they want freedom to teach the Corsican language (Corsu) in schools, and to have more law-making and tax-raising powers. The government in Paris, however, is wary of giving more autonomy to the island, fearing that if Corsica is allowed to break away, Brittany and Alsace might follow (see §88).

The most notorious incident in the recent Corsican nationalist struggles was the so-called *affaire de la paillote* in 1999: in this, balaclava-wearing guerrillas stormed a beachside *paillote* (shack-restaurant) and torched it. As it turned out, the men in balaclavas were in the pay of the chief of police, and the blowing up of the *paillote* was part of a dirty tricks campaign to discredit the nationalists. The corruption went so deep that in the end Prime Minister Lionel Jospin was implicated, and the *affaire de la paillote* contributed to his first-round elimination as a Socialist candidate in the 2002 elections, following which he announced his immediate retirement from politics.

74

Watch *Plus Belle la Vie*

Plus belle la vie does not showcase French culture at its finest. However, it's watched by a fifth of the population, is on the air five times a week, and is, frankly, indispensable to anyone wishing to understand the French. Even if they are French.

Plus belle la vie (which translates roughly as 'Life is Sweet', but doesn't actually make sense, even in French) is a soap opera following the lives of several Marseilles families. The storylines divide into two camps: love and crime. The inhabitants have an extraordinary amount of sex and get into an extraordinary amount of trouble with the police. Sometimes they have an extraordinary amount of sex with the police. If you think *EastEnders*, then add the eternal sunshine of *Neighbours*, and then drench it all with the ambience of anything with Ray Winstone in, you will get the idea.

The set is built around a town square and a café

bar, and features a multicultural cast: the Marci family, owners of the bar; the Torres family from Spain; the holocaust-surviving Mrs Leserman; the Nassris from Algeria; the chronically *déraciné* Chaumette family from Paris; the Estèves, with their homosexual son; and the Frémonts, with their lesbian daughter. Naturally the show has had its first gay-man kiss and first lesbian kiss, exciting horror and saliva in equal proportions; in fact, in its ten years of broadcast everyone has now had sex with everyone else, except Mrs Leserman.

Naturally, this being France, the show has attracted some heavyweight *intello* analysis. One critical insight came from Michel Maffesoli, Professor of Sociology at the Sorbonne. 'The show plays on the dark, evil side of things – crime, delinquency, multiple sexuality,' he said. 'It's an interesting sign of the evolution of French society. France was afraid to show darkness. France is the country of the Enlightenment, and enlightenment means: what isn't dark.'

French Language

75.

Use Litotes

The English think of themselves as the masters of understatement, but the sad fact (for the English) is that when it comes to litotes the French completely outclass them. Or to put it another way, the French aren't at all bad at understatement.

The various French phrases that you will encounter again and again until your brain is beginning to develop an internal shrug, include *pas mauvais* (not bad), *pas mal* (again, not bad), *pas b*ête (not stupid), *pas con* (not a fool), *il n'est pas antipathique* (he's not obnoxious) and *pas dégueulasse* (not disgusting). These actually mean, in turn, pretty damn good, bloody brilliant, that's freaking genius, he's a god, and mmmm, scrumptious!

As with many things, the French look to their literary heroes for guidance. One of the most famous use of litotes in French literature comes from the play *Le Cid* by Pierre Corneille (1606-84). In it, the hero, Don Rodrigue, kills the father of his lover Chimène. Chimène is understandably upset, but tells Rodrigue: 'Va, je ne te hais point' ('Go, I don't hate you'). In other cultures this would be considered a mixed message, but in France it's very encouraging, not to say a little sluttish.

Le Cid was a very controversial play for other reasons, chiefly its unusual dramatic structure and combination of comedy and tragedy. It was heavily criticized by the Academicians of the time, which must have made Corneille think he was really getting somewhere.

76.

Read *Gargantua and Pantagruel*

Gargantua and Pantagruel is a novel – though to call it a novel is stretching things a bit – written in the mid-sixteenth century by the doctor and monk François Rabelais. It is one of the masterworks of world literature.

Gargantua and Pantagruel are two giants, father and son. The five books of their adventures stand at the beginning of a tradition of erudite nonsense later ornamented, in the English-speaking world, by Sterne, Swift, Carroll and Joyce. Gargantua's codpiece takes twenty-four yards of wool to make; when he pisses it drowns 260,418 Parisians (not including women and children); 11,900 pounds of rhubarb are required to ease his constipation; 17,913 cows must supply milk to wean him. Pantagruel can cover an army by sticking out his tongue; with one fart he engenders 53,000 dwarves, which are sent to live on an island where they fight flocks of cranes; there are several cities in his mouth.

In places, it's quite revolting. Here is Gargantua specifying the best way to wipe your arse:

> I say and maintain, that of all *torcheculs*, arsewisps, bumfodders, tail-napkins, bunghole cleansers, and wipe-breeches, there is none in the world comparable to the neck of a goose, that is well downed, if you hold her head betwixt your legs.

77.

Revere the *Prix Goncourt*

The *Prix Goncourt* is France's version of the Booker Prize. Except it's much, much more important than that. The Goncourt was founded in 1903, not in 1969, like the *arriviste* Booker. The Goncourt is named after a famous writer (Edmond de Goncourt), not, like the Booker, after a food manufacturer. And the Goncourt has a small prize of something like 10 euros, whereas the Booker has a big bloated prize of £50,000. The Goncourt trades on the prestige it confers on its winners, which actually makes them richer in the long run. Every Goncourt winner becomes a guaranteed millionaire through the book sales the prize generates.

How much, much more sophisticated.

Winners of the Goncourt have included most of the major names of French twentieth-century literature: Marcel Proust (who won it for À *l'ombre des jeunes filles en fleurs*, the second volume of À *la Recherche du Temps*

Perdu, in 1919), André Malraux (who won it for *La Condition Humaine* in 1933), Simone de Beauvoir (who won it for *Les Mandarins* in 1954) and Michel Houellebecq (who won it for *La Carte et le Territoire* in 2010).

Rules forbid that the award be given twice to any author, but the rules were broken in the case of Romain Gary. Gary was a novelist, screenwriter, aviator and war-hero who netted the prize in 1956 for *Les Racines du ciel*. However, in 1975, a writer called Émile Ajar won for *La Vie devant soi*. This was later revealed to have been Gary writing under another name, a fact unknown to the Goncourt judges. For several years Gary's cousin's son, Paul Pavlowitch, masqueraded as the true author; Gary revealed the truth in a suicide note in 1980.

78.

Abbreviate

❧

The French have a mania for making things *tout court*. In this they are rather like the Australians. Where in Australia an afternoon is an 'avo' and a refugee is a 'reffo', in France an *intellectuel* is an *intello* and a vétérinaire is a *véto*. Other examples are *dico* for *dictionnaire* (dictionary), *dirlo* for *directeur* (director), *bolcho* for *bolchevik* (Bolshevik), *hôsto* for *hôpital* (hospital), and my favourite, *coco* for Communist. And let's not forget Sarkozy, who becomes *Sarko*.

The 'o' suffix is not the only method of abbreviation. Truncation is another popular tactic. So *après-midi* (afternoon) becomes *aprèm*; *petit-déjeuner* becomes *p'tit-dé*; *bon appétit* becomes *bon app*; the *Boulevard Saint-Michel* (the thoroughfare in Paris) becomes the *Boul'Mich*; *d'accord* (OK) becomes *d'acc*; *extraordinaire* becomes *extra*; *en flagrant délit* ('in flagrante delicto', or caught with one's trousers down) becomes *en flag* (obviously a phenomenon common enough to merit a way of saying it quickly); *mais enfin* ('but' or 'come on, give me a break') becomes *m'enfin*; *nescafé* becomes *nes*; *Institut d'études politiques de Paris* (Paris Institute of Political Studies) becomes *Sciences Po*; and *Vélodrome d'Hiver* (the former cycle track in Paris frequented by Hemingway, or *Hémo*) becomes *Vel'd'Hiv*.

Much of the time, Anglo-American words are shortened, leading to some interesting (to our ears) neologisms: bulldozer becomes *bull*; coca-cola becomes *coca*; football becomes *foot*; McDonald's becomes *McDo*. For sailors, spinnaker becomes *spi*.

In other words, a possible sentence in French reads: *Cette aprèm j'ai vu une chose extra: Sarko en flag dans le Boul'Mich!*

79.

Speak in *Verlan*

✺

Verlan is a species of French 'backslang'. It originated among the young, the criminal element and in the music and film industries, and in recent years has moved more and more into mainstream speech. '*Verlan*' itself is an epitome of the way *verlan* works: it comes from *l'envers*, which means 'reverse'. If you split *l'envers* into two halves, *l'en* and *vers*, then put them the other way around, you get *vers-l'en*, or *verlan*. It's more to do with pronunciation than writing. Sometimes syllables or letters may be added or dropped, making it an art rather than a science.

The words that are commonly '*verlan*ized' tend to be those dealing with sex, drugs, race, crime and the police. So, for example, *arab* is *beur*; *joint* (for smoking) is *oinj*; *femme* (woman) is *meuf*; *fête* (party) is *teuf*; *flic* (police officer) is *keuf*; *méchant* (wicked, awesome) is *chanmé*; *louche* (bizarre, suspicious) is *chelou*; *calibre* (gun) is *brelica*. *Verlan* words will often be versions of words that are already slang words, and thus impenetrable to those not in the know (which of course includes most foreigners): *cablé* (trendy, cool) is *bléca; bloqué* (caught, stymied) is *kéblo; jobard* (insane, mad) is *barjot; fais chier* (annoying, boring) is *fais ièche; dingue* (crazy) is *geudin; mec* (guy, bloke) is *keum; gonzesse* (girl, chick) is *zesgon;* and *poulet* (slang for a police officer, literally chicken) is *lépou.*

The point of *verlan* is to hide what you are really saying, so sometimes *verlan* words that have entered the mainstream have been re-*verlan*ized to encrypt them once more. You'd have thought this would just turn them back into themselves, but the transformation process doesn't quite work like that. Thus *beur* (*verlan* of *arab*) is re-*verlan*ized to make *rebeu;* and *keuf* (*verlan* of *flic*) becomes *feuk*, which has a satisfying ring to it in a law-and-order context.

Ce verlan est très bléca.

80.

Know your *Argot*

✾

In French, slang is known as *argot*. Of course, we have this word in English too, where it may sometimes be pronounced with a hard 't'. In English, 'argot' means any specialized language, slang or otherwise – so we can refer, for instance, to the argot of socio-philosophers or bookbinders. In France *argot* just means slang.

Verlan, as we have seen, is a division of *argot*. So is *louchébem*, which originated among French butchers and made its way into general parlance. In *louchébem*, everything begins with the letter 'l', and you form words by inverting existing words and adding end-syllables: so, for example, *garçon* is *larçonguesse*, *monsieur* is *lesieurmique*, and *café* is *lafécaisse*.

As always and everywhere, the purpose of *argot* is not merely linguistic inventiveness but concealment. Children, prisoners, thieves, etc. wish to hide information from parents, warders, the police, etc. Butchers wish to hide information from their customers. So *argot* begins on the streets and works its way up. The surprise in France is quite how far it works its way up. On the grounds of general *égalité*, everyone in France wants to have a share in the *cachet* of *argot*, and everyone uses it, including the social elite, business leaders, politicians and so on. So one might hear a cabinet minister saying:

C'est chouette, cette boum! – This party's a blast!
Je ne peux pas le blairer. – I can't stick him!
Je commence à avoir les crocs, moi. – I'm getting peckish.
J'ai besoin de m'en jeter un derrière la cravate. – I need a drink.

Thus the streets are kept perennially busy inventing new terms to confound their social betters.

81.

Quote from the Fables of La Fontaine

❄

The fabulist Jean de la Fontaine (1621-1695) is probably the most widely-read French writer of the 17th century. This is saying something, because the 17th century also produced Moliere, Racine, Corneille, Perrault, Boileau and Cyrano de Bergerac.

None of La Fontaine's fables is original – they are all derived either from Aesop or other writers of antiquity – but then again, none of the plays of Shakespeare is original. What La Fontaine did was to re-tell these seemingly artless stories in French rhyming verse, and to do it with such adroitness and humour that they are still quoted today. It's sometimes said that you read the fables three times: once as a child, for their freshness and simplicity; once as an adult, for their clever construction; and once as a senior citizen, for their wisdom about the human condition. Well-known *Fables* include *La cigale et la fourmi* ('The Ant and the Cicada'), *L'âne vêtu de la peau du lion* ('The Ass in the Lion's Skin'), *Le renard et les raisins* ('The Fox and the Grapes'), *La grenouille et le rat* ('The Frog and the Mouse'), *Les grenouilles qui demandent un roi* ('The Frogs Who Desired a King'), *La Poule aux oeufs d'or* ('The Goose that Laid the Golden Eggs'), *L'homme entre deux âges et ses deux maîtresses* ('The Man with Two Mistresses'), *Conseil tenu par les rats* ('The Mice in Council'), *Le lièvre et la tortue* ('The Tortoise and the Hare'), and *Le rat de ville et le rat des champs* ('The Town Mouse and the Country Mouse'). Very soon after their creation in the mid-17th century they entered the school curriculum, where they were learned by rote, and thus took the royal road into the French consciousness.

> *L'homme est ainsi bâti: Quand un sujet l'enflamme*
> *L'impossibilité disparaît à son âme.*

Man is made thus: when something fires his mind
Impossibilities are left behind.

82

Read something by Boris Vian,
Vernon Sullivan or Bison Ravi

... who are all the same person. Boris Vian was in fact one of the most bizarre spectacles of modern French life. To call him a 'writer', 'musician', 'dramatist', 'poet', singer-songwriter', 'critic' or 'engineer', all of which he was, seems inadequate; so 'spectacle' will have to do.

Vian was born in 1930 and died at the age of 39 in 1969. He is probably best known for his 'Vernon Sullivan' books, which include *J'irai cracher sur vos tombes* ('I Will Spit on Your Graves'): Vernon Sullivan was a black American writer who Vian had invented and claimed to be translating. The hoax went undetected for years, during which time Vian successfully published three further Sullivan novels, all in a style which might be described as James M Cain meets the Marquis de Sade (he wrote the first one in 15 days). He also published several novels under his own name, the best of which is probably *L'Écume des jours* ('Froth on the Daydream'), which contains a character who has a water-lily growing in her lung.

Vian was an intimate of Jean-Paul Sartre and Simone de Beauvoir, and contributed to their literary-philosophical magazines; Sartre responded by contributing to Vian's marital break-up. Vian was also an accomplished jazz trumpeter and member of the *Hot Club de France*, and arranged for the visits of several American jazz musicians to Paris, including Hoagy Carmichael and Miles Davis.

Vian died in a cinema during a screening of a film version of *J'irai cracher sur vos tombes*, and his last words were reportedly 'These guys are supposed to be American? My ass!' before he succumbed to cardiac arrest.

'Bison Ravi', an early pseudonym, is an anagram of his name. It means 'Delighted Bison'.

83.

Say *Merde* for Good Luck

Merde, of course, means 'shit', although in France it does not quite have the four-star taboo status that English-speakers bestow on the word. *Merde* is probably closer to 'damn' than to 'shit', and is heard in a wide variety of contexts.

One of the most unusual is when wishing someone good luck, particularly in a theatrical performance. Where in English one says 'break a leg', in French one says *merde* or *je vous dis merde*. In the febrile world of the stage, to actually say 'good luck' to someone is to wish enviously for their downfall and writhing failure; and so to wish them a shit performance removes any suspicion of hidden malignity. Similarly one might wish someone *merde* when they have to compete in a race, do an exam or insert a particularly large suppository (see §39). When Moses went up the mountain to receive the Ten Commandments, any Frenchman present would have said *je vous dis merde*.

In speech, if one wants to ring the changes, one might say *je vous dis le mot de Cambronne*. This is in reference to Pierre Cambronne, one of Napoleon's generals. The story goes that when heavily outgunned and ordered to surrender by the British, Cambronne replied with the single word *merde*. The response was made famous by Victor Hugo in his novel *Les Misérables*. One can substitute *Cambronne* for *merde* in any context in which *merde* can be used: thus 'I trod in some Cambronne' or 'I went to see *Les Misérables* – it was a pile of Cambronne.'

You can also say *Mercredi* (Wednesday) as a euphemism.

84.

Learn Some *Contrepèteries*

The French enjoy filthy banter, as any British person might suspect. The very sound of their language is lascivious. And the filthiest aspect of it is the word-play the French call *contrepèteries*. You have been warned.

Contrepèteries means literally 'counter-farts', which sets the tone. Essentially it involves the uttering of sentences which, with a slight shift of consonants, vowels or syllables, would be extremely rude. The effect is like a vile cryptic Spoonerism. Among the oldest of *contrepèteries* is that of Rabelais: *Femme folle à la messe* ('woman crazy at Mass'), which becomes, when the consonants are swapped over, *Femme molle à la fesse* ('woman with a soft *derrière*').

Some other examples: *Toutes les jeunes filles doutent de leur foy* ('All girls doubt their faith'), which becomes *Toutes les jeunes filles foutent de leur doigts* ('All girls fuck with their fingers'); *Le temps abolit les mythes* ('Time abolishes myths'), which becomes *Le temps amollit les bites* ('Time softens cocks'); *Quel beau métier, professeur* ('What a beautiful profession, teacher'), which becomes *Quel beau fessier prometteur* ('What a promise of a beautiful arse'); *D'une pierre deux coups* ('Two birds with one stone'), which becomes *D'une paire de couilles* ('One pair of balls'); and *J'aime vachement ton frangin* ('I really love your brother'), which becomes *J'aime franchement ton vagin* ('I honestly love your vagina'). In conversation, *contrepèteries* might sound somewhat perplexing, until you understand what the speaker is really saying. If you can slip a seemingly-innocuous phrase into a sentence that will only explode with obscene resonance much later, when the lady in question is wondering exactly why you love her brother, so much the better.

The satirical newspaper *Le canard enchaîné* (see the next section) runs a regular column featuring highly inventive *contrepèteries*.

85.

Read *Le Canard Enchaîné*

Le Canard enchaîné is France's version of *Private Eye*. It is considerably senior to Ian Hislop's organ, however, having been founded in 1915. *Le Canard enchaîné* is indispensable reading for anyone who wishes to understand French politics, business and social affairs.

The name *Le Canard enchaîné* is a multi-layered pun. It literally means 'the chained duck', but *canard* can also mean a newspaper, a rumour, or a falsehood. *Enchaîné* refers to a previous newspaper, *L'homme libre* ('The Free Man'), which, when forced to close because of censorship, re-appeared as *L'homme enchaîné* ('The Chained Man').

Le Canard enchaîné is published every Wednesday as a broadsheet consisting of eight pages. As in *Private Eye*, the pages are a mixture of political leaks, satire, cartoons and parodic nonsense, and the newspaper has its own argot, in-jokes and nicknames.

During the post-war period, Charles de Gaulle, nicknamed *Badingaulle*, was a frequent target of the *Canard*, and is said to have remarked every Wednesday: 'Que dit le volatile?' ('What's the bird saying?'). Later Presidents also had nicknames: they include *Sarkoléon* for Nicolas Sarkozy and *Monsieur Royal* for François Hollande (a reference to his longstanding partnership with minister Ségolène Royal).

Among celebrated *Canard* columns are *Sur l'Album de la Comtesse*, which features a *mélange* of *contrepèteries* (see the section above); and the two most ludicrous utterances of the week, the *mur du çon* ('wall of the arseholes') and *noix d'honneur* (a play on *bras d'honneur*, an insulting sign in French, *noix* meaning both walnut and idiot).

86.

Defend the Tongue

The French are well known for their resistance to creeping Anglicization. This has a very long history. The body tasked with championing and defending French is the *Académie française*, which was set up in 1635, when the thing to resist was not English but Italian.

In the modern era the *Académie* is known for its suggestions for alternatives to pernicious Anglo-American neologisms, recommending, for example, that a post-it note should be referred to as a *papillon*, an email as a *courriel*, marketing as *mercatique* and an airbag as a *sac gonflable*. The *Académie* has strong grassroots support from lobbying groups such as the *Association pour la Défense de la Langue Française*, who are rather like the English societies who go around correcting greengrocers' signs with marker pens.

Then there is the Toubon law of 1994, which

mandates the use of the French language in all government publications, advertisements, workplaces, legal contracts and state schools. The Toubon law is also known as the 'Allgood law', since 'Toubon' sounds like *tout bon*, which can be translated into English as 'all good' – which is funny, because 'Allgood' is English.

The *Academie française* receives additional support from a rather less august body, the *Académie de la carpette anglaise*, which could be translated 'The Academy of English Doormats'. Rather like the Ig Nobel Prize Committee, this alternative *Académie* awards an annual wooden spoon to public officials who have distinguished themselves by their un-Gallic spinelessness, allowing foreigners to trample all over the tongue of Voltaire. Recent nominees have included the hapless Claude Simonet, president of the French Football Federation, who adopted the Jackson 5's 'Can You Feel It' as the anthem for the national team, and Claude Allègre, the former Minister of Education, who averred that 'French people must stop considering English as a foreign language.'

87.

Embrace English

However, the picture is complicated, and the good and bad aspects of Anglicization are hotly debated. Take the Toubon law for example (see above), which mandates among other things that all academic conferences should be conducted in French. What does this mean when many participants at French conferences are international scholars who speak no French? One commentator famously said that the Toubon law would turn French academic life into 'five Proust specialists sitting around a table'. (Naturally, many members of the *Académie française* would prefer it this way, and would lay on the *madeleines* free of charge.)

Nor are the Anglophobes getting their way when it comes to promoting French alternatives. Language evolves in an unpredictable manner and the young don't always hang on the lips of the *Académie*. It's not just a matter of *le weekend* any more. The irresistible gravitational pull of the Anglosphere means that English words are not only entering the language by the dozens every year but are being used in ways that the English themselves would be perplexed by. Take the spate of borrowed '-ing' words for common activities. For example 'footing', which in French means 'jogging'. *Veux-tu faire du footing? Oui, bien sûr.* Similarly a shop that advertises 'pressing' is actually offering dry cleaning. A *relooking* – it should be in italics because it's not English at all – is a makeover. And a 'smoking' is a tuxedo or dinner jacket, from the original 'smoking jacket' but truncated in the French manner (see §78). The adoption-plus-truncation strategy also gives us words such as 'baskets' for training shoes (via, one presumes, basketball shoes).

Occasionally an English word, lovingly borrowed, is given a *relooking*, both syntactic and semantic. 'People', for example, becomes *pipole*, which is then applied not to people in general but to celebrities, as in 'the beautiful people'. Then it's turned into a verb, *pipoliser*, meaning to treat as a celebrity, and then a new noun, *pipolisation*, or 'celebritification', particularly of politicians.

Que pense-tu de la pipolisation de Sarko et Ségo?

88.

Celebrate your Regional Language

It is something of a myth that there is a single French language. Unlike in England, where English holds total sway, in France there are multiple Frenches.

The total population of France is currently 66 million, of whom 3.5% – 2.2 million people – speak minority languages. These are not dialects – France has plenty of those – but real, separate languages. The biggest minority language is Alsatian, with around 750,000 speakers, followed by Breton, Corsican, Occitan, Basque, Gallo, Catalan, Franco-Provençal, Italian, Tahitian, Ligurian, Portuguese, Romani, Vlaams, Luxembourgeois and others. Speakers of these tongues are all are becoming more vocal in demanding their rights.

The reality of French linguistic diversity has traditionally been denied and suppressed by bodies such as the *Académie française*. And it's not difficult to see why: the competing ethnic and linguistic groups in

France could, if given due deference, lead to the balkanization of the country and its ultimate dissolution. So runs the argument, anyway. In the past this has led to much injustice, such as Breton schoolchildren being forbidden to speak their own language in the playground.

One touchstone in the controversy is the European Charter of Regional and Minority Languages. France signed this treaty in 1999 – a bit late – but failed to ratify it, meaning that the French government has no responsibility to protect and cherish its native languages, leading to much regional disgruntlement, torching of cars, etc.

It's a French paradox of the type that should by now be familiar. The *République française* is a singular and indivisible State proudly unified under the French language, of course; yet it is also composed of a patchwork of chippy principalities that spent most of the Middle Ages shedding one another's blood and who are not quite able to quite forget the fact.

89

Swear like Captain Haddock

Archibald Haddock is of course the sea-captain in *Les Aventures de Tintin*, famous for his distinctive style of cursing. Hergé did not invent this particular idiom – a mode of abuse in which the sound of the word is more important than its offensive content. Hergé himself was Belgian, but this style of denigration it is widespread thoughout the Francophone world. English-spreakers couldn't call someone an 'hydrocarbon' or a 'brontosaurus' without seeming less insulting than puzzling, but for the French, the essentially tangential nature of the curse gives it its invective heft. Consider, for example, the following Haddock curses (and use them yourself):

> *anacoluthe* ('anacoluthon')
> *autodidacte* ('autodidact')
> *amiral de bateau-lavoir* ('boat-washing admiral')

bachi-bouzouk ('bashi-bazouk')
brontosaure ('brontosaurus')
cercopithèque ('cercopithecus')
coup de Trafalgar ('disaster')
cow-boy de la route ('roadside cowboy')
crème d'emplâtre à la graisse de hérisson ('cream of a greasy hedgehog')
espèce de loup-garou à la graisse de renoncule de mille sabords ('type of werewolf with the buttercup fat of a thousand ports')
garde-côtes à la mie de pain ('breadcrumb coastguard')
hydrocarbure ('hydrocarbon')
lépidoptère ('lepidopterist')
marchand de guano ('guano-seller')
mérinos mal peigné ('badly-combed sheep')
phénomène ('phenomenon')
sous-produit d'ectoplasme ('ectoplasmic by-product')

And, of course, the ultimate insult: *végétarien*!

French Sports and Entertainment

90.

Try *Savate*

In the Tintin adventure *Flight 714,* Professor Cuthbert Calculus (in French, Professeur Tryphon Tournesol) is revealed to be an exponent of *savate*: in a bid to demonstrate his mastery of the art, he launches a mid-air kick that dislodges the entire contents of his pockets, triggering a small hailstorm of pens, keys, watches, cuffs, buttons, money and notebooks.

This sport was not invented by Hergé. *Savate* (or, in full, *boxe Française savate*), is a real and popular French martial art, and is unusual in that it owes nothing to the fighting traditions of the Far East. It was invented in the early nineteenth century by Charles Lecour and Michel Casseux (a pharmacist also known as *le Pisseux*), and originated from the street-fighting techniques of Marseilles sailors. In *savate*, both the feet and the hands are used to launch blows, but the kicking element of *savate* is its most recognizable characteristic, and developed because under French law the closed fist was regarded in law as a deadly weapon. Typical *savate* kicks include the *fouetté* (roundhouse kick) and the *chassé* (piston-action kick): the most painful and retirement-inducing kick is undoubtedly the *chassé italien*, which is aimed at the inner thigh of the opponent, but in such a way that the toe is pointed directly at the groin. Thus *italien*, since even the French wish to dissociate themselves from it.

One etymological note: *savate* derives from the *sabot*, or boot used while fighting. The English borrowed the word to create 'sabotage'. A practitioner of *savate*, or *savateur*, may thus also be a *saboteur*, especially if his kicks land in the most vulnerable parts of the human anatomy.

91.

Hate *Les Bleus* (until they win)

By any standards the French national football team are a success; certainly more so than the English one. *Les Bleus* won the World Cup in 1998, then won Euro 2000, and got to the final of the 2006 World Cup, narrowly losing to Italy. And they have a positive function as role models, acting as a showcase for multi-ethnic France: the widely-used slogan is *Black, Blanc, Beur* ('Black, White, Arab'), showing the three major ethnic identities of France working together.

However, the French regard their team with a contempt they otherwise reserve for civil servants and English cooking. A survey in 2013 found that 82% of respondents had a 'negative opinion' of *Les Bleus*, calling the individual players 'overpaid' (86%), 'stupid' (85%) and 'rude' (73%). These figures were actually worse than those achieved by François Hollande, who is thought to be the most unpopular French president ever. In one notorious incident in

2010, which cemented their image as millionaire divas, all 23 players went 'on strike' following a dispute between Nicolas Anelka and the team's manager, and the entire national side was suspended.

The multi-ethnic harmony aspect is also wearing decidedly thin. The racial make-up of the team is endlessly analysed, drawing the criticism of both left and right; and then there's the matter of the *quenelle* as performed by players such as Anelka, Samir Nasri and Mamadou Sakho, about which the less said the better. It sometimes seems that the role of football in France is to exacerbate racial tensions, not dissipate them.

Perhaps the problem is that although the French team perform creditably at an international level, they haven't pulled off anything really spectacular for a while, and French football fans, unlike their English counterparts, have a low boredom threshold. It will take a big win before the French rediscover their affection for *Les Bleus*.

92

Immerse Yourself in the Ninth Art

The 'ninth art' is the French term for comics. It seems to have been coined by the critic and historian of cinema, Claude Beylie, in 1964, and developed by the Belgian artist Maurice De Bevere, the progenitor of the *Lucky Luke* series. Essentially, the arts, in order of development, according to this scheme or its variants, are 1) architecture, 2) sculpture, 3) painting, 4) dance, 5) music, 6) poetry, 7) cinema, 8) television and 9) comics.

The most common name for comics in France or Belgium is *bande dessinée* (drawn strip), or *BD* for short. Where the Americans or British speak of comics, the French speak of *BD*. French people love *BD*, and France/Belgium forms the third largest market for comics in the world after the US and Japan. It's not just for children, of course: adults consume novels, biographies and pornography in *BD* form; a *BDSMBD* is exactly what you think it is.

The two most famous Franco-Belgian *BD*s are Hergé's *Tintin* and Goscinny/Uderzo's *Astérix*, but there is a universe of alternatives. The third most influential and loved artist in the field is probably Jean Giraud, better known as Mœbius (Mœbius as in 'Mœbius strip' – geddit?). An artist of diverse talents, he is known for his minutely detailed, hallucinatory sci-fi landscapes with series titles including *Le Garage Hermétique de Jerry Cornelius* ('The Airtight Garage of Jerry Cornelius') and *The Incal*.

Who else? Claire Bretécher, of course, with her *Les Frustrés* ('The Frustrated Ones'). Jean-Claude Forest's *Barbarella*. Jijé's *Jerry Spring*. Jacques Tardi and his *Les Aventures extraordinaires d'Adèle Blanc-Sec* ('Extraordinary Adventures of d'Adèle Blanc-Sec', set in an early-20th-century alternative Paris). Marcel Gotlib's *Fluide Glacial*. The magazine *Métal Hurlant* ('Screaming Metal') with its bizarro-gothic feel.

The French idolize their BD artists so much that a popular TV series called *Tac au Tac* ('Tit for Tat') featured artists such as Bretécher, Giraud, Gotlib, Jijé and others drawing cartoons together on big pieces of paper, usually in complete silence.

93.

Try *Joute Nautique*

For this, some knowledge of the TV show *Gladiators* would be helpful. You may recall the segment where the gladiators tried to knock one another off a high perch armed with an oversized cotton bud. *Joute nautique* (water jousting) is similar.

The sport is practised all over France, especially in Languedoc and Provence, but also in the Rhône Valley, Alsace and Brittany. Two decoratively painted boats filled with white-clad figures approach one another on a river or lake: jutting from the prow of each boat is a long wooden structure like a ladder, on the end of which is a platform, on which stands the jouster. The jouster holds a shield and a lance, and as the two boats get within striking distance, the jousters battle to knock one another into the water. In-boat bands play reed instruments and drums. If no 'kill' is achieved, the boats pass one another again. Every time a jouster falls into the water there is a cheer.

It seems that the sport may date back as far as the Romans. In the early 1st millennium there are records of mock naval battles taking place in specially flooded stadia, which included a form of *joute nautique*. The earliest records in France are from the 12th century, and in the 13th, knights, training for their holidays in Palestine, are depicted taking part in water jousting. This is one of the oldest continuously documented sports in Europe.

The best place to watch *joute nautique* is probably the town of Sète in the Languedoc-Roussillon region, which holds a five-day *Fête de la St Louis*, attracting *joute nautique* practitioners from all over France.

94.

Relish Boulevard Theatre

✹

Boulevard theatre is not street theatre in which white-faced persons try to entertain café audiences without the impediment of talent. It is a hallowed tradition of theatre-based performance named after the Boulevard du Temple in Paris, where most of Paris's theatres were situated from the 18th century onwards. This is the theatre of Marivaux, Feydeau (he of the farce), Labiche, and their modern successors. British readers, for purposes of comparison, could think of Sheridan and Fielding, then make their way via Noel Coward to Alan Ayckbourn. Imagine Ayckbourn in French. The middle-class milieu; the social embarrassment; the cuckolded husbands; the French windows (real ones in this case): this is boulevard theatre.

Boulevard theatre has had an enormous cultural impact in France, particularly on film. Hits like *La Cage aux folles* (1978) and *Le Dîner de cons* (1998), and, more recently, François Ozon's runaway success *Potiche* (2010), all owe a great deal to boulevard theatre.

But of course, and wouldn't you just know it, the French critical establishment and *les intellos bavards* (the equivalent of our chattering classes) are extremely snobbish about boulevard theatre. The genre and its filmic treatments are widely considered a blight on French dramatic creativity. Boulevard theatre is superficial, safe, antiquated; and worse, its existence shows that French taste is actually appalling. Perhaps French critics have never really got over *La Nouvelle vague* and that wonderful time when Truffaut came along and conspicuously avoided making any films about bed-hopping Parisians delivering witty lines while being locked out of their hotel rooms with no trousers on.

In short, while in France, go and see a boulevard theatre play – but book in advance, because they are terrifically popular with non-intellectual French people and there will be lines around the block.

95.

Pass a Sleepless Night
in the Name of Culture

❋

The *nuit blanches* (literally 'white nights') are night-time festivals of the arts. Originally inspired by St Petersburg's white nights, they have now become a quintessentially Parisian event. During a *nuit blanche*, from 7pm to 7am, the entire city turns into an art gallery. Museums and exhibition spaces are open all night long, and on every street corner artists ply their trade for the entertainment of the many-headed. There is dance, theatre, poetry, video, installations, light shows, audience-participative performances, and music. The Arc de Triomphe may blossom with weird skulls, or a pack of stilt-legged aliens may emerge from the Panthéon having just consumed the corpse of Victor Hugo. The artists are international and world-class. The secret of enjoying a *nuit blanche* is just to wander and be surprised. Transportation runs for most of the night, but you may wish to stroll until the sky bleaches and you begin to bump into people going to work.

The first *nuit blanche* was held in 2002, and was the brainchild of Jean Blaise, founder of the *Centre de recherche pour le développement culturel* (Centre for Research into Cultural Development). *Nuits blanches* are now held annually on the first Saturday in October, and numerous cities throughout the world have followed suit, with some European capitals teaming up to create a joint project, *nuits blanches Europe*.

The venues in Paris change from year to year, but there is always something happening at Pigalle, Batignolles, Montmartre, and around the Hôtel de Ville. The effect is like being plunged back into the artistic Paris of the 1920s and 30s, only with giant video screens.

96.

Go Crazy for *Les Chansons à la Con*

Anyone who claims the French have terrible taste in music will have no difficulty adducing evidence. Ridiculous novelty songs are enormously popular in France and are known as *chansons à la con* or 'idiots' songs'.

There are various categories of these questionable productions. First there are the parodic songs, usually from stand-up comedians and TV or radio presenters, often featuring *beaufs* (from *beau-frères*, or brothers-in-law, vulgar lower-class sport-loving males with mullet haircuts); then there are novelty dance songs such as '*La danse des canards*' ('the Duck dance') or '*La chenille*' (think 'The Birdie Song'), much enjoyed at lower-class weddings; then fake boy-bands (the Bratisla Boys or *La bande du carré blanc*); and finally the ever-popular accordion-and-beret atrocities (e.g. *Les Musclés* or *Bézu*), a stereotype the *rosbifs* think they invented to mock the French but the French actively enjoy in order to mock themselves.

Exponents of the *chanson à la con* include Sébastien Patoche, a *beauf* character who released a classy number called 'Quand il pète il troue son slip', which roughly translates as 'When he farts, he rips his briefs'; Lagaf', whose 'La Zoubida', a song about a North African girl and some motorbike thieves, was accused of racism and stayed at number one in the French charts for three months; and Carlos, a chubby entertainer much beloved of children whose lyrics ('Big Bisou') are full of worrying *double entendres*.

These songs, with their bouncy basslines and frankly unbelievable videos will invade your mind and stay there forever; so it is highly recommended that you never listen to them.

97.

Go to a *Feria*

❋

Feria...? Surely this belongs in the forthcoming tome, *How to be Spanish*? But no. In southern France, the French word for festival, *fête*, is replaced by the Spanish word *feria*. These southern festivals have a very cross-border flavour. Particularly when it comes to matters taurine. In the southern French *ferias* of Nîmes, Dax, Arles and elsewhere, we find bullfights, the running of bulls, displays of horsemanship, shouts of '*ole!*' and other activities we would more closely associated with tauromachy, Spain and the Spanish.

In Nîmes, for example, during the *Feria de Pentecôte* (Festival of Pentecost) at the end of May, the bull dominates the city life for several days. There are bull runs and *abrivados* (a Provençal term denoting a bull-run accompanied by riders on horseback) in the streets of the city, and *novilladas*, or bullfights, twice a day in the Roman amphitheatre. There is also the *pégoulade*, or opening parade of the *feria*, with its *bandas* (competitive musical groups), and various concerts and firework shows; *bodegas*, temporary bars set up in the streets, slake the thirsts of the million or so revellers. If you can't get to Nîmes in May, try September, when a re-run of the event takes place, featuring identical bulls, *bodegas*, and *bandas*: the *Feria des Vendanges* (Harvest Festival).

The animal-rights aspect of bullfighting is a matter of hot debate in France. Protesters descend on all the major events, and violent confrontations with bullfighting *aficionados* are common. The culture clash is extraordinary. Protesters from Paris might as well be from Greenland as far as their appreciation of the *corrida* is concerned, and the inhabitants of Dax or Arles regard their northern brethren as effete metropolitan fools who have no business trying to interfere in their traditional way of life.

In between the two camps are the American tourists paying homage to *le sport de Hemingway*, and who are quite rightly despised from both sides.

98.

Throw a Menhir

Menhirs are the large pointed stones carried by Obelix, friend of Asterix in the famous comic books by Goscinny and Uderzo. Obelix is a 'menhir delivery man', a joke suggesting that everyone in the little Gaulish village needs regular deliveries of these massive granite objects as if they were pints of milk, despite the fact that Panoramix the druid (Getafix, as we know him) admits at one point that no one actually knows what they are for.

Obelix is often seen to be throwing menhirs. In one notable instance he does so to 'cure' Panoramix, who has lost his memory after Obelix has previously thrown a menhir at him (in the book *Le Combat des chefs*). And in Brittany today one may also participate in menhir-throwing. The World Menhir-throwing Championship, in fact, takes place every year in August, in the Breton village of Guerlesquin, not too far from the village of indomitable

Gauls that still holds out against the Roman invaders. More than a thousand people and journalists come together to celebrate and fling rocks. There are four competition categories: the *Idéfix* (or Dogmatix, for children) category, the *Falbala* (or Panacea, for women), the *Astérix* (for young persons) and the *Obélix* (for adults). The menhirs weigh in respectively at 10, 15, 20 and 25kg. Magic potion and boar, roasted whole in the approved manner, is supplied, all washed down with Breton cider, or you prefer, goat's milk.

The current record in the adult category is an impressive 17.26m.

99.

See something with Louis de Funès in

French cinema and television is particularly rich in comic performers. Emerging from music-hall and theatre in the 1930s, the first great comedic generation included such international stars as Fernandel and Jacques Tati, but many others never made it into the Anglophone world and remain lionized only at home: they include Bourvil, Coluche and Louis de Funès.

De Funès, in his day, was France's leading comic actor, appearing in over 130 films between the 1950s and 1980s. His *La Grande Vadrouille* was, until 2008, the largest-grossing French film ever made. An incensed Chaplin, a hyper-manic Peter Sellers, nicknamed 'the man with forty faces per minute' because of his Tourette's-like expressive energy, de Funès has no real equivalent in any other cinematic figure. In a typical role he produces bizarre and unexpected vocalizations, mimes blowing up his own head by self-inflating his own nose, takes numerous pratfalls, and gives vent to uncontrollable gusts of exasperated rage, usually directed at a straight man such as Bourvil. Short and balding with a giant hooter, he was emphatically not leading man material, but like Norman Wisdom, managed to generate a romantic interest anyway. He worked for most of his early career as a pianist, and played the piano to great effect in many of his roles: his wife, Jeanne Barthelémy de Maupassant (a descendant of the famous short-story writer) said she was attracted to him because 'he played jazz like God'.

Perhaps the best place to start a de Funès love affair might be the comedy with Coluche, *L'aile ou la cuisse* ('The Wing or the Thigh'), a satire on the relations between French and US food culture in the 1970s.

100.

Watch TV – to Better Yourself

'Consonant please Carol...' Could there be a more British utterance? It may then come as a surprise to learn that *Countdown* is French. Yes! *Countdown* is actually a carbon copy of a French game show called *Des chiffres et des lettres* ('Numbers and Letters'), which first aired in 1965 and is one of the longest-running game-shows in the world. Bernard Renard, its numbers genius, is the French equivalent of Carol Vorderman or Rachel Riley; he joined the show aged nineteen, having won twelve consecutive competitions, since short of banning him there was no other way to stop him destroying the morale of any subsequent competitor.

Des chiffres et des lettres is joined by various other programmes that stimulate the little grey cells. One of the foremost is *Questions pour un champion*, first broadcast in 1988. Essentially a quiz show, the questions are set somewhere at *Mastermind* level; not as easy as *The Weakest Link* and not as hard as *University Challenge*. As with *Des chiffres et des lettres* the show has given rise to numerous parodies, such as *Questions pour du pognon* ('Questions for the dough') by the comedy troupe *Les Inconnus*, in which, in one episode, a contestant with no arms presses the buzzer by head-butting it until he covers himself in his own blood. *Questions pour un champion* is hosted by Julien Lepers, a living treasure whose in-your-face delivery and ebullient posturing are widely caricatured (he also looks uncannily like the American actor Michael Keaton). Lepers is much, much more than a presenter: he has written and recorded various pop songs, including 'Je t'aime trop' ('I love you too much') and 'Flagrant délit' ('Caught in the act'), which seem thematically related, and a book on French linguistic usage, *Les fautes de Français? Plus jamais!* (Mistakes in French? Never Again!)

101.

Encourage Guignol
to Beat the *Gendarme*

✺

Guignol is the French version of Punch and Judy, and derives essentially from the same source, the Pulchinello character of the Italian *commedia dell'arte*. Guignol was invented by a part-time dentist in Lyon, Laurent Mourguet, who devised the puppet-show as a way of distracting his patients from the battlefield of tooth extraction. His humanism paid off: the Guignol shows soon proved more successful than the dentistry, and he was able to become a full-time puppeteer, passing the business on to his children and grandchildren.

Guignol appears in the miniature box-theatre we are familiar with from Punch and Judy, and has some of the same stock characters: we have Guignol's wife Madelon, plus a *gendarme*, Flageolet, who Guignol always outwits. There is also a drunken cobbler called Gnafron, Guignol's co-conspirator.

The action is a mixture of slapstick and satire: Guignol epitomises (literally) the small man, the puppet in the street, who manages to get the better of authorities and bigwigs. He speaks with a distinctive Lyonnais accent, vocabulary and humour (boys and girls are called '*gones*' and '*fenottes*', for example).

There are now many Guignol troupes throughout France, and even a macroscopic *Théâtre Le Guignol* in Lyon, with proscenium arch, orchestra pit and all the trimmings. Here you can see adult shows as well as children's, including one in which Guignol repudiates Madelon and negotiates a *pacte civil de solidarité* with Gnafron.

Guignol is not to be confused with *Grand Guignol*, the 'Theatre of Blood' that existed in Pigalle until the 1960s.

102.

Kiss Fanny's Bottom

There are various kinds of games in France that involve throwing balls: *pétanque, jeu provençal, sport-boules, boules lyonnaises*, and others. *Boules* is the less formal name for pretty much all of these. They all involve throwing a series of balls so as to be closer to a smaller wooden jack or *cochonnet*. They also share something else, in that the loser in these games must *embrasser fanny*, or 'kiss Fanny's bottom'.

Kissing Fanny's bottom signifies not merely that one has lost, but that one has been humiliatingly defeated, scoring no points at all – in *pétanque*, to lose 13-0. A loser in this case is himself 'fanny' ('*il est fanny*') and to prove this he is required to kiss a pictorial or sculptural representation of a woman ('Fanny') bending over with bare buttocks exposed, planting his lips on the area indicated, accompanied by ribald cheers and men tooting on bicycle horns. Fanny is an icon in Provence, a true pagan goddess, who crops up in pottery, photographs, figurines, paintings and drawings, and can be seen at *boulo-dromes*, seaside resorts and gift shops.

The original Fanny was possibly a waitress in a cafe in the Dauphiné in the south-east of France in the early 1900s. The story goes that she was in the habit of offering her cheek (that is, of her face) for the losing *pétanque* team to kiss. However, she had a grudge against the mayor, and when the mayor was on a team that lost 13-0, she disdained to offer her cheek, instead lifting her skirts and presenting her posterior. The mayor, a man of imagination, took up the challenge and planted a resounding kiss there.

It's not only the British who can turn disaster into triumph.

ALSO BY ALEX QUICK

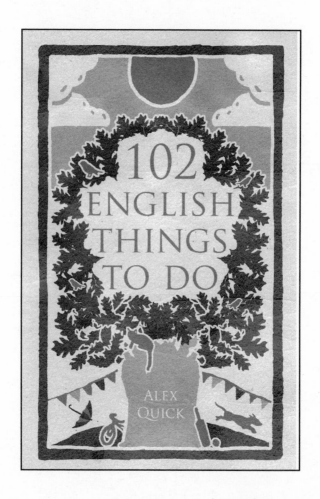

102 English Things to Do / £8.99